I MEANT TO MARRY HIM

BY THE SAME AUTHOR:

WHEN THE WEATHER'S CHANGING
1945

Numerous books for children including

A SPECIAL PROVIDENCE
1964

LIZ
1965

HAL
1975

THREE'S COMPANY
1978

I MEANT TO MARRY HIM

A Personal Memoir

by

JEAN MACGIBBON

With a Foreword
by Robert Kee

LONDON
VICTOR GOLLANCZ LTD
1984

ACKNOWLEDGMENTS

Nine lines from "O Love, the interest itself is thoughtless in Heaven" and one line from "September 1, 1939" both taken from *The English Auden: Poems, Essays and Dramatic Writings 1927–1939* by W. H. Auden, edited by Edward Mendelson, are reprinted by permission of Faber and Faber Publishers and Random House Inc. Two lines from "Times" taken from *The Father Found* by Charles Madge are reprinted by permission of Faber and Faber Publishers. One line from Stephen Spender's "After They have Tired of the Brilliance of Cities" taken from *Collected Poems 1928–1953* is reprinted by permission of Faber and Faber Publishers and Random House Inc. One line from "Villanelle" taken from *Poems* by William Empson is reprinted by his permission and that of Chatto and Windus, Ltd. Five lines from C. Day Lewis's "The Nabara" taken from *Overtures to Death* published by Jonathan Cape Ltd. is reprinted by permission of A. D. Peters & Co. Ltd. Two lines from "A Shropshire Lad" (authorised edition) taken from *The Collected Poems of A. E. Housman* (copyright 1939, 1940, © 1965 by Holt, Rinehart & Winston, copyright © 1967, 1968 by Robert E. Symons) is reprinted by permission of The Society of Authors, Jonathan Cape Ltd., and Holt, Rinehart & Winston, Publishers.

British Library Cataloguing in Publication Data
MacGibbon, Jean
I meant to marry him.
1. MacGibbon, Jean 2. England—Biography
I. Title
941.082'092'4 CT788.M/

ISBN 0-575-03412-2

Phototypeset by Tradespools Ltd, Frome, Somerset
Printed in Great Britain by
St Edmundsbury Press, Bury St Edmunds, Suffolk

"At once I marked him down; I meant to marry him. This simple certainty filled me with a sense of direction which gave point to every moment of the day... I knew what I needed though I hardly knew what to do with it when I got it."

For the Grandchildren

CONTENTS

LIST OF ILLUSTRATIONS

Following page 90

Following page 138

Our honeymoon, 1934: 'The Wolseley Hornet bumped us across France at top speed'

Windrush, Inkpen, on the Berkshire Downs, 1935

Oswald Mosley leads a demonstration in London's East End, 1936: 'We joined the Communist Party' (*BBC Hulton Picture Library*)

Jean Varda with his South Seas outrigger, Cassis, 1937. Roland Pym on left

Painting by Julian Trevelyan of the view from his studio

Julian Trevelyan in his studio, Durham Wharf, Hammersmith, 1936

My sister Ferelyth: 'She forged her own tools'

Varda's boat at Cassis: Michael Higgins, Julian Trevelyan, Roland Pym, Joan Higgins

With Janko Varda, Cassis 1936

Hamish modelling for a Morton Sundour advertisement, 1938: 'All his toys were wooden and educational' (*photo Scott Bushe*)

May Day rally, London, 1938 (*BBC Hulton Picture Library*)

Janet at Abbey Farm, 1939

Abbey Farm

James on manoeuvres

With James fifty years later (*photo Veronica Henriques*)

ACKNOWLEDGMENTS

So many people have helped me to write this book in various ways that I can only mention a few.

I should like to thank Magnus Linklater, whose publication in 1975 of my piece in the *Sunday Times Colour Magazine* series "First Love", was the germ of the book; and I am grateful to Times Newspapers for permission to reprint most of it. Special thanks are due to Nonie Wintour, Patricia Parkin and Frances Partridge for re-reading the manuscript at various stages. Also to my aunt, Ethel Murray, for her specialist advice on the musical life of the period which she and my mother shared. And to Leslie Bedford and his wife Lesley for similar help which only they could have given.

In addition thanks are due to Noël Annan, Veronica Henriques, Hope Leresche, Michael Lane, Robert Kee, Edward Thompson, Julian Trevelyan (for photographs in particular), R. A. Usborne and Peter Vansittart. Hugh Thomas's *The Spanish Civil War* was invaluable for checking my references to that conflict.

I would also like to thank my sister Ferelyth and her husband Bill Wills for many of the photographs reproduced in the book.

It is customary to end with "and last but not least my husband etc". But in this case the book is as much his as mine, the work equally shared, the drudgery falling on him.

J.M.

FOREWORD

by Robert Kee

"THOUGH I MADE them laugh, I embarrassed them, made them uneasy, an aunt has since told me, staring unsmiling, sizing them up." This is Jean MacGibbon's description of her effect on her family as a child and it encapsulates much of her special quality as a writer—a quality with which she herself has lived on uneasy but compelling terms for many years. In this book she has turned that gaze, sinewy with humour, upon as much of her life as she can bring herself to face. Though she ends it over forty years ago, it is nevertheless a complete autobiography in the sense that it is a full portrait of the author and of an essential part of her time rather than just a catalogue of events. It also most subtly contrives to be the honest story of a good marriage, the last forty years of which are virtually unchronicled.

The very fact that her narrative stops abruptly at the beginning of the Second World War is in itself a sort of coded revelation of the autobiography. For before that war had ended, writing under her maiden name of Jean Howard, she had already published stories in *Penguin New Writing* and *Folios of New Writing* and, in January 1945, published a novel, *When the Weather's Changing*, praised by the established critics of the time as "clever", "striking", "altogether likeable", and "full of promise". The novelist Henry Green wrote to her about it: "It is intensely alive and that is worth every other gift in a writer. You are a genuine artist who enriches one's experience . . . at the moment a very good writer indeed and as you keep it up and get to know more about your effects you will be superb." Earlier in 1942 he had picked out her first published short story, "Pension Bellevue", from the pile of manuscripts with which aspiring young authors bombarded John Lehmann's magazine *New Writing* in those years. When a review by her of his own novel

Concluding appeared in 1948 in the other great literary magazine of the period, *Horizon*, he wrote to tell her that, with the single exception of the critic Walter Allen, this was "the only time I've seen anything printed about my work which remotely attempts to describe what I'm trying to do." He added that she herself wrote "like an angel . . . but not often enough." There had been a long story of hers in the distinguished literary miscellany *Orion*, in 1946, among contributions by Elizabeth Bowen, Cecil Day Lewis, Laurie Lee, Edith Sitwell and Stevie Smith. But from 1948 onwards, from the writer Jean Howard, there was nothing until now.

It is true that about ten years later, when I happened to be Literary Editor of the *Spectator* for a time, I persuaded her to write some reviews for that paper, which she did with professional accomplishment. Other papers such as the *Sunday Times* and *Observer* recognized this and also published her reviews. And in 1959, under her married name, Jean MacGibbon, she began to write children's stories which were published with some success. But these were essentially the products of an able craftsmanship, to which that unsmiling writer's gaze, which could quite disturbingly make you laugh, has been fairly ruthlessly subordinated. Now this book, she tells me, is "instead of all the stories and novels I ought to and perhaps might have done".

What had happened?

I had long ago been given a clue, towards the end, in fact, of the very year in which her novel was published, 1945. She had arrived for lunch one day at the house in which I was living in Regent's Park and, to a complete stranger who opened the door to her (myself), could talk of nothing but the (to her) appalling fact that bread was being cast carelessly upon the waters of the Park lake for ducks and other birds to consume at their whim. That aberration of the mind's mechanism which can cause it to use its focussing powers to distort rather than illuminate reality, and the literally indescribable pain this causes the person whose mind it is, was doubtless already at work within her. That Jean MacGibbon so successfully battled over a number of years against bouts of what is euphemistically called mental illness is a tribute both to her courage and to her intelligence. The illness receives no attention here, but to the fact that she did so battle, as also to the fact that she had to, we owe this slightly strange autobiography— fragmented, dislocated at times, but also a fascinating whole.

On one level it is an interesting and often charming photograph album, providing random glimpses into cultured middle-class family life of the inner and outer London suburbs in the second and third decades of this century, and later into amateurish though dedicated political involvement in the nineteen-thirties. As with all photograph albums the coverage is uneven. The former period receives more detailed "sizing up" than the latter though the captions are always good: "There is cruelty in clinging to a false view of anyone"; "In the Communist Party there were restraints that suited me" etc.

On another level this book seems to me to essay that most difficult but worthy of all autobiographical tasks: rejection of an apparent outer coherence in favour of a search for those many inner fragments of which one's human personality is somehow mysteriously composed.

On both levels Jean MacGibbon seems to me to be that "genuine artist who enriches one's experience" discerned by Henry Green more than forty years ago.

Robert Kee

I MEANT TO MARRY HIM

I
Golders Green

My Golders Green, where I lived till I was twelve, was all green dusted with buttercup yellow, a little furred at the edges, contrasted with dark, jungley Weybridge where I was often sent to stay with my father's parents. I hated that featureless name: "Hampstead Garden Suburb". My Golders Green was a safe, sunny, open place bounded to the east by Wild Wood and Big Wood where in spring revels were held called "Sanfairyann". Near our house was Wild Hatch where the nursery garden grew, smelling of sweet damp earth and young growth. Southwards rose up the forests of Hampstead, forbidden ground haunted by bad men, a Highwayman and a Headless Coachman. To the west, trim houses, each bounded by pale-green hedges square-clipped to a given height, opened on the Finchley Road where trams vented their tropical-birdlike screeches and the North London Underground, then at its terminus, continually swallowed and voided passengers.

Our Heath was the Hampstead Heath Extension, a pastoral slope of fields, hedges and trees whose turf washed the walls and watchtowers of a citadel crowned with the spire of Saint Jude's Church like a Rhenish town. Over us all brooded the spirit of Dame Henrietta Barnett who had designed the all-embracing noble plan of the Suburb. She ordered the innocent pattern of our lives, shielding us from the corruption of the material world: shops were forbidden within the confines of the Suburb; as to pubs, none of us would have entered one had they been allowed. She it was who laid down what plants were to be grown in squares and public places—magenta Rugosa roses in odd corners, yellow standard roses in our square garden, William Allen Richardson pink climbers on the pergola overlooking the crematorium, favourite meeting place for nursemaids and prams. ('There goes another poor soul!' as a column of brown smoke rose in the still air.)

Class distinctions were observed: rich people lived in the long-windowed Lutyens South Square where Saint Jude's sharp spire over against the benign dome of the Free Church symbolized more than ecumenical accord. Here education was cared for by the Institute and the Dame Henrietta Barnett School where the girls wore scarlet flannel pinafores embroidered with a daisy. "Nature I loved, and next to Nature, Art", as we were reminded by roads named after painters—Linnell Close, Constable Close, Reynolds Close. We lived in the middle-income area in a square bisected by a road leading on to the Heath. To the north, artisans were provided with model cottages and gardens in roads with Anglo-Saxon names like Asmun's Way.

For me the heart and centre of Golders Green was my mother's Bechstein piano. No one was allowed to touch it; she polished it herself with an old silk blouse. She was a pianist, an accompanist and singing teacher. She was full-breasted, with large grey-blue eyes and thick, dark hair, waved over her temples, coiled at the nape of her neck. Her forearms were full and rounded, her hands remarkable, shapely and strong, yet so worked on to keep them supple that you could have shone candlelight through them. Her fingers were the colour of the ivory keys, shell-pink at the tips. When she played, what she did with her fingers on the keys was more like my idea of making love than anything I have since experienced. I had some idealized fantasy of love-making in my imagination, some precocious knowledge of sex, perhaps from earliest memory, from birth, and her playing fulfilled it.

Sometimes I could not bear her playing. No doubt I had my share of the jealousy of my father that boys, more than girls, are said to suffer from; but the Bechstein, like a lover, was the worse rival. Together my father and I competed against it for her attention.

My mother would not have understood this sexual fantasy, this obsession of mine; it would have disgusted her. Piano-playing was her work, wholly realistic. She would have understood better my personification of the composers she played. Bach, for instance, was a reassuring friend from earliest memory and I had a clear idea of what he looked like, formed not from portraits but from his sound and shape as he and she worked together. Another favourite was Scarlatti, specially when she played what I called his "hunting song", high treble thirds, crisp as late apples in the first frosts, loud to begin with, then echoing through the woods. When I first read "*Dieu que le son du cor est triste au fond des bois*" it was that music I recalled. At the time the music had been joyous; only later the memory was sad.

Chopin I both loved and hated, receiving from him prematurely a fatal notion of romantic passion. This is no comment on Chopin or my mother's playing: it is what I made of them. The two of them carried on an intimate dialogue excluding the world, excluding me. One piece was specially disturbing, beginning not on what I thought of as "middle C" (the tonic) but a third above, on no particular note, as though they were carrying on where they had left off the night before.

Sometimes I banged on the floor after I was in bed, complaining, when my mother came up, that her playing was keeping me awake. She would nibble my ear-lobes, lick the sides of her spatulate thumbs and smooth my eyebrows.

The music did not begin again.

She herself did not much like being touched, at least not grabbed at. She suffered, perhaps, from hyperaesthesia, possibly because of injuries suffered in an early accident (it was her right arm I remember seizing, and her sudden pain). This seems at variance with my recollection of her muscular arms, her strong frame. But that it was true was confirmed by my father who, when he was near death, stopped me when I made to put a hand on his brow: 'You remember how Mother hated being touched?'

She was born in Ayrshire, Margaret Murray, towards the tail-end of a family of formidable women and one boy, the youngest. They moved to Glasgow where their father was a sugar merchant, a sugar grinder, no-one would tell me what exactly he did. Their fortunes seemed to ebb and flow along with sugar, that unstable commodity.

Because of an accident when she was two which left her with

one blind eye, a broken arm and a broken leg that took three years to heal, she was kept a good deal at home. From her earliest memories she felt happiest sitting at the piano; and when she was five Thorpe Bates, a singer who taught at the Glasgow Athenaeum, heard her and recognized her exceptional talent. She was given a scholarship, and taught by Philip Halstead, then at the beginning of his career as a pianist. By the time she was eight she had become a child prodigy, ripe for exploitation by her parents. She did not, she said, suffer from those early concerts; it seemed natural to her to play wherever she was, and she felt no apprehension about playing a Mozart concerto in Saint Andrew's Hall with the Scottish Orchestra. As a result she had little formal education. Her sister Sibell remembered her sitting up reading in bed, a hand covering her blind eye, ready to blow the candle out at the sound of their mother's step on the stair.

At fourteen she won a scholarship from the Royal College of Music in London to study in Leipzig; when she was old enough to take it up her parents found out the name of a German *Pension* and put her on a boat bound from Leith to Hamburg.

My father and I never tired of re-living, of agonizing over this part of her story, of how this lovely sixteen-year-old girl with dark hair coiled under her sailor hat, half-prostrated by seasickness, was set down at night on the quayside of the German port. (Daddy used to grind his teeth at this point . . . 'How could that ignorant pair . . . I blame her father most!')

Some kind man put her in a cab which deposited her with her box and her tartan valise on the doorstep of the *Pension*. A maid, startled by her sudden appearance, showed her straight into a dining room where a hundred young male faces turned upon her—it was a boys' school!

Next day she was sent on to Leipzig. From then on her time in Germany, in spite of hardship, was all satisfaction. Leipzig was at the height of its musical reputation, with the conductor, Nikisch, Principal of the Conservatoire. On her first morning she played for Teichmüller, head of the piano department, who took her as his pupil.

She was extremely poor; even in those days five pounds a month, including the hire of a piano, was not much to live on.

So she looked after children in the afternoons. Here she was fortunate: they were the children of Charles Spearman, the philosopher and psychologist. She was taken into the family; and Fanny Spearman remained a close friend after their return to England. Young Margaret Murray brought back from Germany more than a musical education; through the Spearmans she was introduced to a liberal society which, she told us, was wider thinking, warmer hearted, more humane than the English middle-class life she entered after her marriage. My mother could never quite come to terms with the kind of society E.M. Forster describes in *Howard's End* and which he contrasts with the German culture of the Schlegel family.

But her time of expansion in Leipzig was cut short: after eighteen months she was sent for to come home. Her father had gone bankrupt, cheated by his son-in-law till the firm was ruined. She arrived home in time to find her mother taking her sister Nellie by her long fair hair, pregnant as she was, and throwing her downstairs. My aunt picked herself up, followed her errant husband to Cape Town where she ran a boarding house, met her second husband and lived happily ever after. Such were the temper and fortitude of the Murray family.

My grandparents looked to Margaret for support. But she was no longer a money spinner, a child prodigy. At seventeen, with her extreme shyness and sensibility, she was ill-fitted to teach in a school; and such engagements as came her way, like playing in concert parties on summer piers, never lasted long. But she kept in touch with her friends and teachers in Glasgow and before long discovered her true métier as an accompanist. When Evangeline Florence, a coloratura soprano of international reputation, came to give a recital in Glasgow, and her accompanist fell ill, she was advised to try young Margaret Murray. She did, and from then on till the singer's death in 1929 the two were never separated for long. Evangeline took her back to London, to her tall house in Kensington Park Gardens which became my mother's natural home, secure in the loving care of Evangeline and her husband, who attended on them both, and read Browning to Margaret when her headaches were bad and she could not sleep. He belonged to the Browning Society, friend of many literary contemporaries. My father disapproved of him because he did no work: he, too, had been the victim of fluctuations in the sugar trade, and lived on his wife's earnings. He was my godfather, an attractive figure in his pepper-and-salt overcoat of fine cloth and brown velvet collar, and brown soft felt hat.

Evangeline depended on Margaret for unremitting work—she taught in addition to her concert performances—and for daughterly ministrations when, an ageing woman towards the end of her career, she was overtired, taxed almost to illness by her continuous engagements. They toured Europe and America; Evangeline was a Bostonian. For perhaps three years my mother lived at the centre of musical life of Edwardian London with all its brilliance and technical accomplishment. Friends abounded—Liza Lehmann, the singer and composer, and her circle, younger friends like Myra Hess and Irene Scharrer. With musicians my mother could be herself, give herself unreservedly in a way she may never have felt free to do in her own family.

One day she and Evangeline went down to Weybridge to see my Howard grandmother, an amateur composer, with the idea that Margaret might give her singing lessons. My father set eyes on her; and never let her go.

For the first six months of their marriage they lived with his parents, a period too miserable for her to talk about. From there they went to a house in Chepstow Villas, Notting Hill Gate, where I was born in 1913, and where my mother could be near her friends and keep up some of the life she had so briefly enjoyed. It was not a life my father could share: they kept irregular hours, came back to the house late after concerts. He remembered Irene Scharrer coming round after they had gone to bed, a fur coat thrown over her nightdress, to continue some absorbing discussion with musical illustrations. Before long he took us to live in Golders Green where the atmosphere suited him as it did me. I am neither a Londoner nor a countrywoman but a suburban at heart, never more content than within walking distance of Hampstead Heath.

My mother loathed Golders Green consistently during our twelve years there. 'Too much high thinking and low living,' she would say, 'too many sour oranges in wooden bowls.' She felt utterly cut off. Yet she entered loyally into the Suburb's activities; played and sang whenever she was needed; and made one or two lasting friends. There, as elsewhere, she was loved and needed; yet this was something she could never believe, even among ourselves. 'I'm just an old boot,' was one of her half-serious rebuffs to our protestations of love. There was a terrible grain of truth in this; for my father and I used her, could not help ourselves.

Every morning my father left the house in his bowler hat, carring a slim leather attaché case on his way to "business"—a confusing term since "doing big business" meant "going to the lavatory". He was above average height, never weighed much more than seven and a half stone, never had a serious illness in his life. He was a chartered accountant, a junior partner in his father's firm, Howard Howes. Every evening he returned drained by the work he hated but did conscientiously. He needed to find my mother at home. I have never understood how she managed to keep up her professional life, having, as a rule, to be back about six. Sometimes she had to take a taxi from Golders Green Underground and must have been loweringly aware of the two of us, Daddy in his corner of the dining room, me crouched on the half-landing, obsessed, at the end of our tether.

But often she could work at home; and often, if she were still engaged with a singer when Daddy came back, after he had changed and stretched himself out on his bed to rest I sat on his bony knees in the dining room, leaning against the rough tweed of an old Norfolk jacket bleached pale as old straw. Near his head was a glass-fronted bookcase filled with the works of Sir Walter Scott, prizes bound in half-leather, stamped with the Harrow crest, books about Scotland, and the Tusitala edition of Robert Louis Stevenson. He cared passionately for Scotland and Scottish history. The rigours of public school life proving too much for him, he had been sent to Saint Andrews to be tutored for Balliol by a young university don, Robert Hannay, afterwards Historiographer Royal for Scotland, and to be mothered by his wife, Jane Hannay, one of the first pupils at St Leonard's school, St Andrews, where it was founded in 1877.

> Saint Andrews by the Northern Sea
> A haunted town it is to me

wrote Andrew Lang. And so it must be for everyone who has lived in that grey, granite, salt-pickled town thrusting ruined towers into the North Sea. There was never any question but that my sister and I should, in our turn, travel the five hundred miles to school there.

He smoked "Three Nuns" tobacco. Names of people and things meant more to me than the objects they represented, and these words recall the sweet, mild smoke that encircled us, a resting place, a brief reassurance of rightness in our world, while someone in the next room sang Vaughan Williams' setting of "Linden Lea". My mother's fingers were like footsteps from one verse to another, leading voice and accompanist along a prospect of autumn-coloured lime trees. A homecoming.

My mother led us all into singing. My father stood by her at the piano, his gentle boyish features scowling, round shoulders squared, his light tenor pitched low, gruff, vengeful.

> Ye ha'e slain the Earl o' Murray
> And ha'e laid him on the green!

Scottish songs aren't all sad, or savage battlecries though he had a preference for these.

She would break into the dashing arrogance of "Leezie Lindsay", the mockery of "The Laird o' Cockpen", the highstepping tread of "Ho ro my nutbrown maiden". There is a Scottish word "jimp" which describes her singing of these lighter songs, trig, delicate, brisk.

Between them they imbued me from earliest memory with Scotland in all her parts and moods, the Highlands, the Borders, lochs, mountains, glens, betrayal and slaughter, the laughter and pain, the fine-footed dancing, the skirling gallantry, the underlying tenderness, the lament for an oppressed but unconquered people.

It comes to me as I write—and it is a leap into speculation—that for my father my mother embodied Scotland as Jeanne D'Arc, for the French historian Jules Michelet, stood for France. It was an extra dimension of my father's passion for her, a source of his idealization, encompassing her victory over physical and psychological injuries which had scarred her for life, her abundance and diversity of spirit, her mockery and anger—and her chancy weather. She was all things Scottish to him, not least in that plain, sound common sense which, traditionally, makes benighted travellers welcome, and made for us a warm home, "a couthy bield".

I think of them and the black Bechstein too big for the small drawing room, singing Gilbert and Sullivan, and songs from the musical comedies of their youth.

One my father specially liked because of the tripping patter:

> Rhoda, Rhoda kept a pagoda (pagoda!)
> Tea and bread and butter and soda (and soda!)
> (etc)
> What pretty pagoda Rhoda ran!

But I liked to hear sad songs, not mournful but reflective.

> Loveliest of trees, the cherry now
> Is hung with bloom along the bough,

my father sang. It was sad for me because a cherry tree bloomed every spring outside the window. At one time the garden had been kept; we had tea on the grass. But after a while it was neglected; no one went into it but the cook, to get coals. The privet hedge between our house and our neighbour's had grown wild and high. But the cherry bloomed as my father sang. My sadness had also to do with the song, the short span of youth, my father's small voice (he could not have sung for anyone but my mother) and his small head, his rimless pince-nez, and my mother's great dark head of hair, her smile as she looked up at him. They were vulnerable; I ached, powerless to protect them. Yet the ache was part of the song.

When my father was not away playing golf, as he did for most of every weekend, he took me for increasingly long walks through a gap between Wild Wood and Big Wood which, then, gave on to open country. When I was confined to a bath chair after some illness he galloped behind my wicker chariot, hallooing at the top of his voice, while I steered the small wheel at the end of a metal joystick; we were Romans in a chariot race.

He taught me to play cricket before I was seven. Captain Danks who lived in Reynold's Close ran a cricket club for his and his neighbours' children. I haunted the outfield on the sheep-cropped turf, as a first-year schoolboy watches the First Eleven, with no more hopeless, high ambition than to belong. My father bought four stumps, a composition cricket ball, a bat signed "Jack Hobbs"; he taught me to play forward, to play back, to keep a straight bat at all times. Impressed, Captain Danks sent round a formal note inviting me to join the Reynold's Close Cricket Team. This was the first of few athletic triumphs, for though my father could teach me style he could not teach me timing and pace. I played six games at school, all stylishly, all enjoyably, none effectively or with distinction.

My father and Jack Braithwaite always reached the finals in the Golders Green Tennis Club tournament, played on two grass courts behind Hirst's garage, their yellowing flannels supported by striped silk foulards. My mother presented the prizes.

The people who lived in Golders Green fell into two categories; those who lived there for cheapness and convenience, waiting for promotion or a father's death, whereupon they would up sticks and make for Central London; and those who meant to live out their lives in Dame Henrietta's demi-Paradise. Among these were the Braithwaites. Although Jack Braithwaite became Sir John, President of the Stock Exchange, the family kept their house in Hampstead Way, adding to it so that the original twentieth-century beamed and plastered building came to look like a seventeenth-century farmhouse with eighteenth-century additions. Their house was a regular venue for parties, and concerts given by our piano teacher. At one fancy dress party Mr Braithwaite was a handsome, swarthy pirate. His wife was dressed as a "Nippy", as Lyon's waitresses were called, in a very short skirt and a frilled cap and apron. Afterwards my mother made fun of Mrs Braithwaite and her skinny legs of which she was envious, having a false picture of herself as grossly fat. Nettie, she said, did not know her age; she had appeared as Pan in the Big Wood spring revels wearing spotted tights and a goatskin (a libellous fantasy). Mother made fun of everyone behind their backs, specially her friends, as she did of my father and me to our faces. It was a way of expressing the irritation we both caused her. She could not help herself; it was part of her talent for mimicry, we understood this and led her on. My father, indeed, may from the first have invited her barbs, for he took pleasure in being a butt and was never tired of telling us how he had been bullied at Harrow, how his brother had made him bend over a fence to be peppered with cat pellets. And I soon learnt to clown. I could not bear my clumsiness, the way things "broke in my hands", my lefthandedness in a family where deft fingers were at a premium. "Being funny" created a diversion.

I was seventeen before it dawned on me that my parents were in some ways ill-suited to one another. Till then I had thought of them as an ideal couple, though it is hard to explain how this view was maintained alongside impressions to the contrary. It was at about that time that I realized that my father's extreme possessiveness linked with his obsessional habits, his overriding need to preserve her energy, not for her own well-being but for his comfort, drove her to the limits of endurance. "It would be too much for her" became a familiar phrase, usually applied to her professional work, the one thing that never made her ill. After her death he told us that Myra Hess had asked her to help with the National Gallery concerts during the war. 'I couldn't let her of course. It would have been too much for her.'

Yet his tender care won her gratitude; and to feel grateful, for her, was to feel loving and giving. They were perpetually engrossed with each other. Sometimes the small house reverberated with altercation as it did with music, and for reasons incomprehensible to children. Once, when we were about to set out on an afternoon's expedition my father came out of their room crying tragically, 'Now we won't be able to have tea in St Albans!' He was an amateur of tea shops as other men are of pubs.

And there are other very different memories: of the two of them walking across the Heath, she with her short legs stepping out to keep in rhythm with his long strides; they sat on the grass beside cropping sheep, her face freckled by sunlight through a basket-weave hat with a wreath of cherries, more delectable than real cherries. Memories of flirtations, gentle love-play, private interchanges whose meaning is known only to husband and wife. Yet I could not share in their happiness, more tormenting to me than their unhappiness since I could not be part of it.

Had it not been for my sister I should have been inclined to discount my version of what went on. But Ferelyth, born when I was three and a half, seems to have known at once that, between the three of us, she had been dropped into a queer kettle of fish. This gave her much unhappiness; but it kept her saner in the long run. Recognition of the truth, however painful, is the foundation of sanity.

We were both grandmothers before we could talk together about our parents, such were the uncomprehended deeps of our feeling as a family. 'I suppose,' she said, 'it was the contrast between so much loving warmth and the rows that went on.'

'Did they go on when I wasn't there?'

Yes, she said, they did, and this was a relief to me, for I had always believed myself responsible; and there was some truth in this since I jumped into the middle, exacerbating the trouble. Ferelyth saw all this going on and felt excluded. Also she sometimes felt guilty at not being able to help me. Had she been the elder of the two our lives might have been easier; we might have made common cause.

My jealousy of her went beyond what is normal and persisted for years. Her being fair, gentle, vulnerable, stirred mixed feelings in which pride and love were submerged, envy uppermost. The singularity of her name was an added injury. I don't know why she was called "Ferelyth", Gaelic for "water-fairy".

My own idea about our parents is that the root of our bewilderment was their true tenderness for one another, and this overlaid by an ideal, false conception of what marriage should be. Had they been indifferent we could have come to terms with it. It was their frustrated love that made us uncertain and insecure.

One unexplained result of my insecurity was that early on I began to feel that I was someone rather special, somehow different from other children. This notion was furthered by the odd solitary life I led on my frequent visits to Weybridge Granny where I was favoured and could do no wrong—but that is to come.

In Golders Green I led the healthy, ordered life of an ordinary little girl, slapping down the clean pavements with my mother on our way to the "village", as the Golders Green shops were called, past uniform hedges and well-kept garden plots. The houses were not uniform: the architects of the Suburb, within guidelines, were given their heads and built in different styles, from Tudor-beamed to Lutyens-Georgian. Our house in Corringham Road, at one end of our half of the square, was faced with a big chequer-board pattern, a semicircular pediment breaking the roofline, as though built of Lott's bricks.

Our way led us past a hexagonal bastion thrown out from a Tudor-style house, wherein lived a mother, recently widowed, and her three willowy daughters, all four with a classic cast of features that would have made them subjects for Julia Cameron's photography. When I first read Tennyson's "Idylls of the King" it was the Taits who came to mind.

I divided my friends into those with whom I did/did not play quasi-sexual games on the Heath, about which I felt a guilt which was worsened by my conviction that my mother had once said: 'I know everything you do. I know at once by looking at your face when you have done something wrong.' She may never have said this: but I believed in her all-seeing eye; yet could not give up my secret life. The Taits were "did-nots". I sensed that they were good. There was a blessed lack of tension in their house, a benign cheerfulness about their beautiful, unselfconscious smiles that was due, I thought, to the absence of men in the house.

At Waitrose's, at the butcher's, the greengrocer's, money rarely changed hands; these shops all gave us tick, though it was not called that. Only Sainsbury's, smelling of smoked bacon forever freshly sliced, where girls in mob-caps, reflected in long mirrors painted with storks and bulrushes, tossed and patted butter between wooden paddles—Sainsbury's, like Boot's, worked on cash. Every month small leather-bound books stamped in gilt with cows, fish, baskets of fruit, were sent up to our house. There ensued a fearful drama called "doing the books", in which every item was scrutinized by my father, my mother called to account—which of course she never could be. She never had a bank account of her own. 'She would have given it all away to her wretched family,' said my father. And perhaps she would have done, with her open-handed generosity. Nevertheless, he might have tried her. It would have given her consequence in that man-made world. As it was she paid for everything "on account", and to the monthly ordeal was added the quarterly trauma when bills came in from the West End shops. She hid them among her gloves, her stockings, scrumpled up at the backs of drawers, staving off the day of reckoning.

Money was only one cause of disharmony; but it was the most obvious one, apart from electric tension at meals because of what the maids might think when Daddy wanted to toast his own toast at the Esse Stove (he had poisoning fears about others touching his uncooked food), or have three sorts of biscuit and other crumbly comestibles all at once on his side plate. Daddy had been brought up never to think about the maids: Mother thought about them a great deal. Apart from catering for Daddy they were her chief domestic preoccupation; she cared for them. And they in turn adored her. She wasn't very good at choosing maids—a cook, a house-parlourmaid, a nursemaid with interchangeable roles—she was easily imposed on. Connie, an excellent worker, disclosed to her that she had an illegitimate child; and for a time this ill-mannered little runt lived in our small kitchen, straying into the dining room where he took a bite out of every one of a bowl of apricots. Some had hysterics. Some fell seriously in love with her. Alice, whom I liked, sat by her packed box with tears running down her starched apron-front. I couldn't understand why she was being sent away.

Shopping, even locally, meant getting away from these cares. We ended our round by changing our books at Boot's library. Mother, who slept badly, even with the help of drugs, read at night, one hand covering her blind eye, and needed new books all the time. The children's section was in a dark corner at the back of the shop, where I found Angela Brazil, Victorians like Henty and L.T. Meade and all the works of Amy le Feuvre, chosen because of the name. Next to Boot's was my favourite shop, Booker's sports shop. Here I had bought for me in turn a scooter, a Pogo-stick, a proper leather football, a Scout pole for vaulting ditches, and in due time a Raleigh bicycle. On the way home we met other mothers for coffee at the Refectory.

When it was not a shopping day Mother went to work with Aunt Evangeline and sometimes took me with her. The 28 bus stood in the Underground station yard with its fan-patterned cobblestones. We swayed and stopped and ground our way through the slums of Paddington and North Kensington to Aunt Evangeline's tall house in Kensington Park Gardens.

My godmother sat in her rocking chair in the middle of her long-windowed music room, bare except for a piano and gilt party chairs against the walls, teaching. She had a small black monkey which sat on her shoulder. The rocking chair, of hickory inlaid with fruit wood, had come with her from Boston when she married Uncle Sandy, a Scot from Perthshire. She was small-boned, her head set on slim shoulders, her hair set on her head like a brown bird's nest. She had quick, dark, brown eyes and sang like a bird, without apparent effort. She was celebrated for the width of her range, and in one song she became a bird. Up she flew, with the flute after her, echoing her song; they echoed each other, flew together high in the sky, or in the rafters of some great concert hall. Evangeline and the other singers who came to her house and ours sang every sort of song, from Mozart to contemporary song-cycles and ballads, with the same care and brilliant technique. This was still the age of sheet music and popular concerts like the London Ballad Concerts at the Queen's Hall in which performers, in addition to their own chosen repertoire, sang a proportion of drawing-room ballads. I sat on the steps of the Wigmore Hall while Aunt Evangeline, wearing crimson brocaded velvet, rehearsed a catch, "Ground Ivy", with a quartet. One of the men was John McCormack. The women were Evangeline Florence and Clara Butt.

There is a gaiety and simplicity among musicians, perhaps because they need to work together strenuously, exactly and in accord. Charm, fun, laughter, these are qualities impossible to make convincing: they don't come off the page; but there was much laughter and simple fun between my mother and her circle. People like Myra Hess, Irene Scharrer, close friends before her marriage, and whom she still met at my aunt's, played childlike pranks on one another, perhaps letting off steam after the tension of performance, which I much enjoyed.

Children have a logic of their own; they accept grown-up behaviour at face-value, but put their own interpretation on it. For instance the singer, Carrie Tubb, one Christmas at home, "swallowed" the silver pig in the Christmas pudding. I took it that she and Clara Butt were sisters, one very small, the other large, as I believed the pig had really been swallowed, and both beliefs an occasion for hilarity. My favourite form of humour was, and still is, the in-jokes, the musical pratfalls, like repeatedly hitting a wrong note at precisely the right moment.

Music itself is full of rollicking humour: there is a bumpity–bumpity bit in Schubert's F major Octet which I liked to hear over and over again. I remember Mother and another pianist playing Johann Strauss's Tritsch–Tratsch Polka at tremendous speed, getting hands and arms entangled but finishing at a triumphant gallop.

At this point in my memories I found myself up against a difficulty: my mother as a working mother came clear at last out of the emotional tangle I had projected on to her. But what about the stories I got her to tell, her way of remembering the pre-war years of concentrated professional life before her marriage? How to make sense of my jumble of names and places—parties at Leighton House, painters, poets, Alma-Tadema, Alfred Noyes, ice puddings like castles, great houses, transcontinental trains with drawing-room coaches and silk curtains with bobbles on them, the American tour, the friends she made in that welcoming country, a church spire at the top of a long hill (Boston), frame houses, views of America, or a part of it, superimposed on pictures from American children's books. Visionary, confused as my version was, its intensity surely derived from her sense that this period of splendour and expansion, in such contrast to her previous life, was compressed into so short a time.

I needed to find someone who had shared something of that pre-war musical life.

One of Mother's most loved older friends was the singer and composer, Liza Lehmann. Reading her book, *Liza Lehmann By Herself*, I found confirmation of the kind of atmosphere I have tried to recapture, which so enchanted me as a child.

I remember that Liza was beautiful, a shadowy yet all-encompassing presence. She and her two sons came to see us at Golders Green; and we visited them at their country house. Her husband, Herbert Bedford, was a painter—he was also a composer but the other aspect is the one I remember. On that visit he gave us a handsome book, *Meredith's Heroines*, illustrated by him with portraits taken from life. I pored over it in my nursery and got to know the pictures by heart so that when I grew up and read the novels Clara Middleton in *The Egoist* and Diana Merion in *Diana of The Crossways* were not strangers to me; I expected his heroines to be outstanding.

Reading *Liza Lehmann*, then, was a confirmation of my version of my mother's memories. But following that came an unlooked-for piece of good fortune: from Rosamond Lehmann, the writer, I learnt that her cousin, Leslie Bedford, Liza Lehmann's younger son, was still very much alive. I wrote to him and he wrote back saying that of course he remembered my mother, 'her fine musicianship and personality'. He had, he wrote, 'vivid recollections of a visit to your house when . . . you sang Vaughan Williams' setting of Robert Louis Stevenson's poem which ends, "And the hunter home from the hill". I have loved it ever since and its comfortable key of G flat.'

I spent an afternoon with him and his wife, the singer, Lesley Duff. He is a distinguished scientist, a mathematician, an electronics engineer. Their three sons are well-known musicians.

From them I learned that the life my mother spoke about was much as she remembered it; nor had I falsified her memories by mine—something it is all too easy to do, devaluing with open mockery or exaggeration another's precious, true lifetime history. I was right, Leslie said, in remembering his father as a painter, and that he had illustrated *Meredith's Heroines*, some with portraits from life. He asked if my mother had not sat for one of the portraits? 'She was very good-looking,' he said.

During our talk I realized that my mother had continued to work as an accompanist and singing teacher longer than I remembered, well beyond the war years and through the twenties till Evangeline's death in 1926. After that she worked less regularly, and almost entirely for friends. This I could have worked out for myself but for my difficulty in trusting my memories of her, particularly as a loved, working, successful mother. Shortly before Irene Scharrer's death—I had written to her and she telephoned me—she spoke of my mother's "genius", adding that she was much loved. I think that when I was very young I could accept her as she was; but increasingly her talent, the aura with which she was surrounded and the love she gave and received led, among other reasons, to terrible difficulties.

But during this golden afternoon with the Bedfords, none of that obscured my happiness. It would have been a joyous occasion anyway. Rosamond wrote of her cousins as "the adorable Bedfords", and I can't improve on that.

When it was time for me to go, Leslie went to the piano and played the song in the key of G flat. And Lesley, his wife, sang it.

> Under the wide and starry sky,
> Dig the grave and let me lie;
> Glad did I live and gladly die,
> And I laid me down with a will.
>
> This be the verse you grave for me,
> Here he lies where he longed to be;
> Home is the sailor, home from sea,
> And the hunter home from the hill.

A strange song, perhaps, for a six- or seven-year old to be singing at parties. But death interested me, and I had picked the song up from hearing it.

Death seems to have been something of an obsession. Mother told a story about my rushing up to her, my little sister in tow, shouting: 'Ferelyth won't promise to put flowers on your grave!' Weeping but adamant, she stood her ground: 'I don't know what a grave is.'

My mother and I loved parties and theatregoing—this was one thing we could share. After an early lunch I would be put to bed, to lie in happy wakefulness in the light of the gas fire, with a full-skirted dress of sprigged organdie or taffeta, tucked lawn petticoat, short silk socks and dancing pumps on a chair near by. Often fog hangs in the room. Washed, dressed, bundled up, I am hurried out to a taxi whose smelly, slippery leather cushions combine with Mother's skunk furs, a bunch of violets pinned on the collar, to create a party mood as we jerk through failing light, muffled up against sulphurous, raw air, on our way to Kensington Park Gardens, where the best parties took place.

As to my singing, there was nothing notable about this: both children and grown-ups sang readily at parties. Though singing at Aunt Evangeline's was far from doing a "party piece".

I must have sung well, as Leslie Bedford says I did, or I should not have been asked. I mostly sang what grown-ups sang, the drawing room ballads, which nowadays seem, some of them, more suitable for a child than an adult. One of them was by Ivor Novello. He had been brought to see my godmother when he was a boy by his formidable mother Clara Novello, and she sang, my mother claimed, his first published song at a London Ballad Concert. As this is something of a curiosity, here it is in full, or a verse of it from memory.

> Little trout among the shallows
> Where the water ripples wide
> Won't you leave your weedy nursery,
> Come with me and spend the night?
> Nurse will give us nice hot water,
> Soap that smells of flowers and things
> And a towel so soft and downy
> You can hear the angels' wings.
> Nurse will (something, something)
> Watch us dry and help us dress
> And you shall sleep behind the pillows
> In the downstairs linen press.

(And then the chorus, "Little trout . . .".)

It's a good tune which I will willingly sing down the telephone to any interested reader.

A song which had a lasting effect on me went:

If no-one ever marries me
And I don't see why they should
For nurse says I'm not pretty
And I'm certainly not good
I shall buy a little orphan girl
And bring her up as mine.

It was the little orphan girl that did it. I had made no plans for marrying and thought it likely indeed, for reasons given in the song, that I never should. But the idea of being lumbered with a little orphan girl was intolerable. At the earliest possible opportunity, I hid behind a Rugosa bush in Hampstead Way, waiting for David Braithwaite. We were both on our way to a eurhythmics class, and can't have been more than five or six as we were dressed in identical holland smocks with peasant embroidery, the only difference being that his knickerbockers showed an inch, mine being elasticated.

'David,' I cried, leaping out as he passed, 'will you marry me?' He stopped dead; looked at the pavement, then at me: 'I shouldn't count on it,' he said. As he was destined for the Stock Exchange I have often thought this early habit of deliberation must have stood him in good stead.

That song did seem to me, in later years, to be pushing the childish innocence touch, typical of many such ballads, a bit far. What was my astonishment to find, when reading Liza Lehmann's autobiography, that the words were by Alma-Tadema, the celebrated painter, the music by Liza herself. Liza Lehmann was a serious composer with a worldwide reputation: according to Groves' *Dictionary of Music*, the founder of the English song-cycle. Admittedly the song was in a group for children. But adults sang it in public. As I grew older "serious" music, vocal music in particular, became extremely "special", surrounded by a holier-than-thou purity: highbrow is the word. From my earliest days I listened inattentively to all kinds of song, Bach, Handel, Mozart, *Lieder*—I'm not sure Evangeline sang *Lieder* but other singers accompanied by my mother certainly did—and the French repertory in which Maggie Teyte excelled. But the songs I remember best from those early days are the English songs, the song-cycles, like Liza Lehmann's setting of Fitzgerald's *Omar Khayyam*, Roger Quilter's settings of Tennyson, "Go not happy day", "Now sleeps the crimson petal, now the white", and the two Vaughan Williams' settings already referred to. The truth is that I was not captivated by "serious" music, never "carried away" as I enviously watch others being, even people who appear to be tone-deaf. Before long I grew fidgetty during the great seasonal festivals that took place in the Albert Hall, Handel's "Messiah" and Coleridge-Taylor's "Hiawatha". To this day I cannot happily sit out an entire concert. By half-time I've had enough.

Sitting on the floor in people's houses was what I liked, free to fidget or even go away unobtrusively. On Sundays Great-Uncle Ernest Howard often arranged for first-rate string quartets to play, except for the second violin which he took on himself, in no way embarrassed by holding them up and having to begin again. He and Aunt Sophy had charade parties during the First World War in their Finchley Road house which shook every time a train ran underneath, and later in their St John's Wood house. Those charade parties continued for many years. They made a gathering point for the Howard clan. Ernest's sister, Aunt Alys Hannay, a painter, was often there in black velvet, diamonds, lace and purple silk stockings, with her speedwell-eyed daughter Katharine, who married the writer Peter Grant Watson. He it was who came upon me, aged six or seven, in my Howard granny's summerhouse reading Ethel M. Dell. 'You'll never be a writer if you read that rubbish,' he said. But had no effect on my low taste, except the conclusion that if I wanted to be a "proper" writer I must at least be *seen* reading "proper" books.

The Ernest Howards entertained a number of writers, painters and musicians who meant little except, as I grew older, for an agreeable sense of moving in a different world from Golders Green. May Sinclair, the novelist, sat absent-mindedly with her dress buttoned on back to front. Aunt Sophy (I believed comfortable sofas were named after her) played the hind legs of an elephant in pantomime, Julian Huxley played God under an umbrella. That was early on and he meant nothing to me. But his father, Leonard Huxley, did because, with his sprouting moustache, he was called "Mossyface".

As well as grown-up parties there were children's parties at which I was shamelessly competitive, ruthless in Musical Bumps, all fingers and thumbs in Musical Parcels, ready to cheat if I could, not noticing the other children much, often ending in sudden collapse, what other people's nannies called "being beside herself".

In those far-off days Fancy Dress parties were the best, for I could act the part. What with war shortages crêpe paper was in demand, daffodils and roses popular; by running a finger nail down a petal clever fingers could make it curl. But our mother, a natural actress herself, provided expensive costumes for us. She bought a crimson, full-skirted dress edged with swansdown for my sister, labelled in the shop as a "powder puff" which she thought common. She changed Ferelyth into a "Christmas fairy". I was a pierrot to match, with crimson pom-poms on my white costume and conical felt hat, and clowned away frenetically, though in "real life" I had mixed feelings about clowns, hated circuses and never laughed wholeheartedly even at Charlie Chaplin, who seemed a caricature of my father at his worst.

Most of these parties were in Golders Green. But much the best party we ever went to was at Greenwich where Erskine Hannay, a Naval cadet, was stationed at the Royal Naval College. As the only son of Jane and Robert Hannay, Daddy's surrogate parents in St Andrews, Erskine was "one of the family". He was tall, dark, permanently sunburned even on the backs of his square supple hands, which made my heart turn over as he played "Dardanella" in a dashing manner, fudging the tricky left hand. I loved him more or less faithfully till his marriage when I was sixteen. As with cousins, "family friends" have great latitude: when be bathed in a lake near London I sat on his shoulders, my hands in his wet curls, till he tipped me in. I sometimes had morning tea in bed with him.

But the Christmas party at Greenwich would have ranked as the best even without Erskine. The occasion was splendiferous, in those great halls designed by Wren, the painted ceilings, the majestic staircase, all crowded with children in every sort of colourful disguise. I took in the splendour, impressed by the general effect, the superiority of the refreshments spread out on long tables in the Painted Hall so vast that the further end was obscured by river fog. But what I homed in on were two muscular ratings in perfectly clean, navy-bordered vests who propelled us down a long chute. I was dressed as an "Eastern princess" in a tight-trousered suit of tarlatan, gold Indian muslin, with a headdress and jewels. When it was time to go home there was nothing to the seat of my trousers but the orange sateen lining. Typically I have forgotten what Ferelyth was wearing. But I remember her glued to a sideshow, a glass goldfish bowl with pennies at the bottom through which a weak electric current had been set up. Ferelyth worked out a way to get the pennies. How? Perhaps she simply fetched her rubber galoshes from the cloakroom. Her interest was partly scientific; she likes to know how things work. Also she early on discovered the value of money and savings, as when she spent most of her time at the Hampstead Fair rolling pennies down a groove until she had perfected the knack.

Fog seemed a part of our Christmas parties and theatre-going, adding to the uncertainty of our arrival with even more exciting speculations in the icy taxi as to the unlikelihood of our getting back. Fog, thick, blue-black, all-silencing as it rolled off the Heath, fog, sulphurous yellow as we groaned past the lighted shops, fog, haloing the lights in the theatre till they were dimmed and footlights dawned on crimson velvet curtains, the audience silenced, the orchestra not too loud to drown the swish of heavy drapes as the curtain rose . . .

I was taken to my first pantomime at a very early age, perhaps by one of my mother's sisters on a visit from the distant parts they mostly lived in, at the Winter Garden Theatre. 'Winter garden, winter garden,' I chanted, drawing from the words a picture of a jungle in a cold climate, struck by an Ice Age. So compelling was my fantasy, all I remember is being high up in a vast, cold cavern, icy with cold air, fringed with jungle leaves, palm fronds edged with ice, through which at an immense distance could be seen a lady in a pool of light singing "I'm forever blowing bubbles".

We—our theatre parties were often shared with our next-door neighbours—were taken to every entertainment suitable for children, from big productions to plays put on in some small theatre like the Everyman in Hampstead. One which I never forgot was *The Soul of Nicholas Snyders*, all scarlet, flame and darkness, frightening as one enjoys being frightened in the theatre. Without understanding all, I understood some lasting truth about the nature of good and evil. (Since writing this I have been told that the play by Jerome K. Jerome was not as serious or frightening as it seemed. Well, it was all these things to me.)

Where The Rainbow Ends, on the other hand, though purporting to be about good triumphing over evil merely, like *Punch* cartoons, assumed an identity between moral feeling and Conservative Party patriotism. As a play it was spectacular, tophole entertainment in which two midshipmen and a girl defeat the Devil, who shot out of a trap door in green armour, with the help of Saint George who appeared from nowhere in a flash of white fire.

The Demon in that fine Thatcherish play had nothing, of course, to do with the Demon King of Pantomime. There was always a good pantomime at the Golders Green Hippodrome in addition to at least one visit to the West End. Pantomime is, or was then, the perfect entertainment for children, with the constant changes of scene and tempo, the knockabout acrobatics, the bellyaching jokes, all of which could be recreated in the nursery. My favourite "Dame" was Nelly Wallace. Her wiry, eccentric cheerfulness, her cocksureness, the stylish assurance with which she adjusted a shawl or hitched up her knickers were the very opposite of what made me unable to laugh at circus clowns with their sad faces and huge painted smiles, always on the receiving end of fate. I could all too easily have become a clown: I could never be Nelly Wallace. But I could and did imitate her, with increasing faithfulness down the years, in charades, at parties, her gestures, her voice, her funny feet; she became my first professional piece of acting.

I come to *Peter Pan*.

As the Greeks were taken every year to be purged by pity and terror, so we were taken every winter to *Peter Pan*. And if there seems to be a ludicrous discrepancy between Aeschylus and

J. M. Barrie, I can only say that *Peter Pan* is my *Oresteia*. Both plays after all, have to do with family life. Peter symbolizes the loneliness of mankind, the prowler, the outcast in all of us, peering through a locked window at an ideal family never to be regained.

Sitting on the edge of my tip-up seat, as always, in Mother's phrase, "with pins in my knickers", there would be no conscious thought beyond the play itself, the glory of it from the moment the nursery walls open to the night skies and Peter flies in. Waitng for Captain Hook to poison Peter's medicine, waiting for the crocodile and the alarm clock, waiting for the joke about Smee and the sewing machine and Captain Hook's breeches, familiarity bred only a heightened anticipation.

A point not generally noted is that Peter is at heart a girl, always, until 1982, played by actresses. He is a girl inside a boy who doesn't want to grow up. I could have played Peter: it was my ambition. The flying, oh, the flying, I could learn. All the other things Peter did I could do. He is not really very boyish; look at the way he struts around, the stance he takes up when grounded. No proper boy stands straddling with his hands on his hips. The only moment when he becomes truly Pan, a moment of thrilling fear, is when he sits cross-legged on the powder-keg, playing his pipes, and the barrel is kicked away and he stays airborne. Otherwise, so closely was I identified with him, I saw no great obstacle to taking his place.

Peter's character is not admirable; he is hardly human. It's not just that he is self-centred, vain, untruthful, posturing: he lacks that most enviable of human qualities, tenderness.

In spite of looking in at so many windows, Peter has no idea how human life works: he doesn't know a kiss from a thimble. Wendy has to teach him how to behave when they are playing at Mothers and Fathers underground. I didn't think much of the fairy Tinkerbell; my clapping to save her life, when the audience had to show they believed in fairies, grew perfunctory as the years went on. But now I see she has significance, this hovering mercurial light with a tinkling hiss like a musical rattlesnake. Tinkerbell knows all about humans. She has common sense. She is not wholly good; she is jealous enough to have Wendy shot by a Lost Boy's arrow, but she loves Peter; she is always with him, ready to protect him with her life. She is a truly feminine part of Peter, a little piece of his mother. When Peter cries out for help to save her his anguish is genuine; for without her he would be lost indeed.

Tinkerbell has her own reasons for egging him on to bring the children home; she knows Wendy and the Darling family will do him no good.

For me the climax of the play came when Peter returns to the empty nursery and hears Mrs Darling playing the piano, breaking off to call out her lost children's names: 'Wendy, Michael, John!'

And Peter brings them home.

I did not care about the rest, the nonsense about Wendy and her spring cleaning and the lights in the trees: 'The mauve fairies are boys and the white ones are girls, and there are some colours who don't know what they are.'

Consider the Darling family: I need not labour the point that they were identifiably my own family. Mr Darling, the breadwinner, something of a figure of fun, sometimes in the doghouse; Mrs Darling and her piano an idealized "good" mother; Wendy my sister, the two boys, perhaps, the sons our parents never had. The double rôle of Mr Darling and Captain Hook, always played by the same actor, is too well recognized to need comment. As to my rôle, it was never in question.

(Our own three children were in no doubt either: Wendy, Michael and John were easily accounted for; Captain Hook/Mr Darling, of course, was their father. And Peter Pan . . . 'Oh, Mummy can be Peter Pan.' Who played Mrs Darling? Another double rôle, perhaps.)

My husband, who never saw *Peter Pan* till he was grown up and took the children, was shocked, revolted. What he minded most was the degrading of the father: 'Cheating, lying about his medicine, being put in the dog kennel . . .' *Peter Pan* leaves most people with strong feelings one way or another.

I had been looking forward to taking the grandchildren, and eagerly bought tickets, But turning away from the ticket office I realized that I myself could not face it: I had had enough of *Peter Pan*.

II
Weybridge

BECAUSE OF MY mother's illnesses or my father's possessiveness, his need to be all-engrossing, I was often sent to my father's parents, who lived in a large, castellated, creeper-covered house in the foothills of St George's Hills.

My mother later told me there was another reason: Granny came and took me away; she would like to have kept me always. Weybridge Granny was enormous, shapeless, but with incongruously small feet on which she tittupped like a top-hampered boat in a sou'westerly. In her embrace I held my breath, deep among silks and floating scarves and silver chains and an unpleasing inner softness.

Sometimes, in the timelessness of childhood, it seemed that I lived there; and was driven up for the day to visit my mother in bright airy Golders Green and the Heath at the end of the road. How was it that, leaving my loved mother, having to stop at the chemist's to have a calming grey powder shaken on to my tongue, lying doggo in my grandmother's embrace under an opossum rug, Hammersmith Bridge arching over our heads in the last of the winter light, acetylene lamps tunnelling through avenues of clipped laurel and dripping sweet chestnut—how was it that I yet felt a kind of release? Perhaps because, at Croxley, nothing was expected of me.

Ears humming in the sudden silence, I stood in the vast hall while Annie, Granny's personal maid, unpeeled scarf and coat and gaiters.

In wintertime, tea was laid by the library fire. Home-made pippy blackberry jam was served in a pot sunk in a silver holder. Granny spooned jam and cream, scalded and skimmed for her alone, on to her toast. After tea she went to work at once making cigarettes for Grandpa, a pink tin of tobacco at her elbow with almond blossom on it and the words "Lambert and Butler". My grandfather had a financial interest in the firm. Whenever possible they used commodities—writing paper was another—in which he had a financial interest. She worked with quick, nervous fingers, teasing the tobacco into cigarette papers, licking, rolling them into a doll-size Venetian blind, snipping, letting the ends like droopy moustaches fall into the *Westminster Gazette* on her stained blue serge lap. My grandfather "had an interest" in the Liberal newspaper. Annie took me up to bed in the night nursery. The house was built round a volume of air, the hall roof-high with a gallery running along one side giving on to the two principal bedrooms and a dressing room, leading under an archway into the billiard room which in turn gave way to the second spare room where my parents slept when they came. The night nursery was connected with this room by a housemaid's pantry that smelled of Brasso and a sodden wood sink. Over the coal fire in the nursery, spurting dragon fire jets of flame, hung a coloured print of Little Red Riding Hood, the wolf's mask lurking in the bushes behind her.

Annie had a funny thick way of getting her tongue round her words. She was Cornish. She had gone out with my grandmother when she and Grandpa sailed to Australia in 1879 in a vessel that was partly under sail, partly under steam. Annie had left St Agnes, come straight to my grandmother and had never left her, a body servant in the true sense. As I remember she seemed not much changed from the girl of seventeen, not in her ways. But she was an old woman, with scurfy sparse hair and a dribble of yellow stuck to one corner of her mouth. I accepted her work-grimed fingers and her ministrations. She was my idea of a witch, but a familiar witch, without occult powers. She was always the same.

Grandpa came to see me before dinner. He had changed from his office clothes into a black velvet smoking jacket. He smelled of Army and Navy soap and a touch of Lambert and Butler's Straight Cut, smoked through an ivory holder that stained his moustache. He was a gentle, sad man.

The Howard family had been farmers for five centuries. But by the time my grandfather, Walter, was born in 1851 the farm had been sold, and my great-grandfather managed a flour mill in

Hertfordshire, a peaceful country of streams and woods and water-meadows where the children grew up happily enough in the tolerant, Liberal-thinking atmosphere of a Unitarian family.

But the mill did not prosper. And when the two eldest boys, Great-uncle Will and my grandfather, left school they immediately set up in London as accountants, Will going about drumming up custom, while Walter stayed in the office doing the accounts. By the time he was nineteen he was able to write to his brother, 'Eureka! We've made a profit of £3000!' In a year or two they had extricated my great-grandfather from his unprofitable mill, brought the family to live in Crouch End, settled the three younger boys at school or in business and had their two sisters suitably educated.

I like the story, so much part of Croxley, I like the feel of it under my feet, the Howard part of me warms to it. No Howard that I have heard of has ever quite lost his head or become bankrupt.

All my great-uncles seem to have used their earnings and their spare time pleasurably and energetically. With their wives and families they painted, made music, designed houses to live in and to sell, and drove those Titans of the antique world De Dion Boutons, Renaults, Panhards, all over the British Isles and Switzerland, secure in their confidence that they would never lose money over a deal.

Only my grandfather was sad, as Daddy never tired of telling us, because he had had to leave Australia. My grandmother could not stand being so far away, her health broke down. 'But why?' Daddy would cry, backhanding his forehead, expressing the anguish his father could never express, 'Why? She had everything. She even had Cecil Sharp at the Conservatoire!' (She composed songs.) My father, born in Adelaide in 1883, remembered the house Grandpa built there, the garden made "with his own hands", horses galloping along endless shores, and how he was taught to swim by being tipped off his father's shoulders into the waves.

So all the joy and all the juice went out of Grandpa when he had to return to London, to the accountancy firm he had founded and the daily journeys to and from Weybridge: his life, with the Liberal Party, the Weybridge Literary Society, the strenuous exercise, was a *tour de force*.

Grandpa had a cold bath every morning in a metal and mahogany bath which thundered when the taps were turned on. Outside the window among the ivy and the sparrows was a ledge where he kept his sponge. But he used the downstairs "doubleyou", as my grandmother called it, a room not for women, smelling of Sanitas, lined with boots, mackintoshes, racquet presses, fishing tackle, at the end of which was a mahogany "t'rone", as Annie called it, with a topaz handle that pulled to open a trap in a man-sized pan decorated with blue chrysanthemums which frightened me as I had once fallen into it, bum down, and had to be unstuck. I was not supposed to be there; but I could do what I chose at Croxley.

Like the downstairs WC, Grandpa's dressing room was lined with boots on wooden trees, leather riding gaiters, leather dumb bells, Indian clubs and a hunting crop. He sometimes rode before breakfast.

While his two sons were still at home the three of them used to bicycle before breakfast to bathe below Shepperton Weir where the Thames meets the Wey, return to breakfast and catch a train to London in time to begin work at nine. The elder, Liddon, worked in Great-uncle Alec's timber business. After my father came down from Oxford he worked for Howard Howes during the day; and until he qualified as a chartered accountant had to work for his exams after the day's work, catching a train back in time for a late dinner.

My grandfather, wanting for his son what he had missed himself, sent him to Oxford where he read history. 'Why, oh why,' Daddy would lament in his old age, 'why *Oxford* when he intended me for the business?' Far better, he said, to have sent him to a French or German university to learn languages. In vain we counterclaimed his lifelong passion for history. He had a clear brain and a retentive memory till the end of his long life, during which, he would remark, he had seen more changes than during the period between Isaac Newton's death and his birth. He would have preferred to be a schoolmaster or a country solicitor. But, perhaps because of some disappointment in his elder brother, he was to succeed his father in Howard Howes.

Weybridge abounded in young men under their father's

thumb, intended for a life they had no choice in, emerging to catch the 8.15 from creeper-clad houses buried in woods where conifer, sweet chestnut and silver birch fought for supremacy, hurrying down tortuous avenues which connected not with each other but with the railway station.

Weekends were no less strenuous. Parties were made up for golf, tennis, boating, dances were held in each other's houses, "surprise parties", theatricals, picnics, girls in huge hats, veils and dustcoats, gently flirtatious, liberated by "the motor", sailing up and down the Seven Hills Road en route for Wisley Lake and the North Downs. My father spoke of these things; I peopled house and garden with his memories; and perhaps came in for the tail-end of that time myself, or its continuation during the War. One Christmas the drawing-room floor was strewn with French chalk, the conservatory lit with Chinese lanterns. The double doors into the back drawing room were opened, and there, in the scent of resin and hot wax, a candlelit Christmas tree soared to the ceiling. Mother played; my father waltzed, upright, arm extended, lightly holding a kid-gloved hand, revolving adroitly among the couples. He waltzed as he skated, in the English manner; with comparable restraint he glided over frozen water-meadows, hands behind his back, inclined slightly to right or left as he described a figure-of-eight.

At that party the hexagonal conservatory with a date palm in the middle smelled of geraniums. The place fascinated me for my father said that people got proposed to in the conservatory. An Oxford friend, he said, Patrick Gordon Walker, (father of the Labour politician), proposed to his future wife among the palm fronds. Daddy, whose tender fondness for women was never indecorous, was attracted to full-blooded, fashionable young men, men who "sailed near the wind" and "got away with it". He delighted in reminiscing about them, his light voice dropping a tone or two, unnaturally hearty, as when he sang vengeful Scottish ballads. He lent his rooms at Balliol to Mr Walker for supper parties, and next morning the room would be strewn with cigar butts, empty champagne bottles, a large photograph signed "*Toujours à toi*, Gertie".

But for the most part we had the house to ourselves, Granny and I, after I had seen Grandpa off, bowler-hatted, striped trousered, to walk to the station. Granny breakfasted in her brass bed hung with white muslin curtains. Wrapped in shawls, she would already be rolling tobacco, newspaper scattered over the bedclothes, all thrown aside as I entered, dived resolutely, breath held, into a vast, soft, shapeless mass, face brought up against her damp, white buttery chin, held there among crumbs of Breakfast Biscuit and tickly tobacco till I could slide to the floor and escape.

When she got up we might go shopping, if it was fine, in "the motor". Or we might set out on a round of "calls", leaving cards if her friends were out. She dressed in an Edwardian style, with large hats, a feather boa, her gloved hand resting on the silver knob of a long-handled, purple silk parasol.

One day the Renault landaulette, with its elegant bonnet like a tropical leaf or lily, emerged from the double garage and was driven away as a contribution to the War Effort. After that they made do with the open, biscuit-coloured Rover, exhilarating in warm weather with its hot leather cushions and shipshape brass, but draughty with the hood up. As a further wartime sacrifice Granny bought a tricycle and I, being four years old, was given a small one. The pedals were on the front hub and as I rode recklessly down the terrace bank, too fast for my feet to go round, the pedals beat a tattoo on my shins. The chauffeur wheeled the big trike to the front door, Granny mounted and was pushed to start along the drive, me with my legs going like pistons after her. We sailed downhill all the way to Weybridge village where we called at the butcher's, the fish shop, to order what was to be sent up. If we were in the motor, Granny did not get out. Shopkeepers came out to her in their straw hats and striped aprons. Pedley and White's was more than a hardware shop to me: there they sold the tarry rope for my swing that was renewed every spring. And above their shop-front was an aeroplane propeller of polished wood, a real one salvaged from Brooklands aerodrome.

On the way back we were met by the Rover. The gardener took over the big trike and mine was put in the front seat.

After lunch Granny went to bed. The whole house was mine, to explore, to chart. At first I took in only separate rooms and what went on in them. Later they became connected. But there were areas of unknown territory that opened up as my legs grew longer. I revisited the stuffed white owl under the stairs, slid through the baize door into the kitchen quarters, past the dark storeroom to which Granny kept the key, doling out candles and brown soap, flour, plum jam, sugar out of a stone jar. In the sunny kitchen Cook slept in a Windsor chair, feet on the fender where bread was rising in a copper pan, while the kitchen maid scoured the table bone-white.

Electricity was generated to serve the house. But the back stairs, uncarpeted, were lit by flickering gas jets at dark corners. These stairs were connected with the bedroom floor through swing doors elbowed open by maids bearing coal scuttles, hot-water cans, teatrays, slop pails. It was some time before I discovered that these stairs ended in the kitchen quarters. Later still I climbed up to the attics where the maids slept on iron bedsteads, each with a strip of carpet on bare wooden boards, a chest of drawers, a shared washstand with enamel basin and slop pail, smelling of the stale sweat that collected underarm in their black stuff uniforms.

Searching these rooms for clues I found nothing, an emptiness that was vaguely disturbing. The maids' windows opened on to the leads, to steeply sloping roofs which, later still, became dangerous Alps to climb, slates too hot to touch with bare feet. From the rooftrees I surveyed the whole garden. Westward lay the front garden, terrace, lawns, and beyond the disused tennis lawn the Wellingtonias and the high-flying, dangerous see-saw. There was my cedar and my swing, the summerhouse, the path that ran alongside the house, past pampas clumps, the kitchen garden, through the wood which belonged to Croxley. Southwards the gravel drive slept in full sunlight; to the left, in front of what had been stables, the Rover was being washed. All round there were woods enclosing more houses like castles in fairy tales. Through treetops arose the campanile of "Olantye", in the Italianate style, where a bell hung with a real rope that descended right through to the hall. Two girls lived there with their father; their brother had been killed in the war. They made teasets out of halibut bones.

If the Bechstein was the heart and centre of my Golders Green, the swing under the cedar tree was at the heart of my

Croxley. After an absence, my first move was round the terrace, down the bank and across the lawns. Swinging there under layered branches dark as malachite, palms roughened by friction against tarry pigtailed rope, I was entirely at ease, leaning back at stretch, hearing above the rush of air the drone of aeroplanes from Brooklands aerodrome nearby. The noise of aeroplanes was a summer sound, as were the noises of hammering, sawing wood, the song of a thrush, perhaps because windows were kept closed in winter. Or because the helmeted men in open cockpits wearing uniforms like smart chauffeurs were grounded more often in bad weather. Above my cedar tree monoplanes, biplanes, Sopwith Camels, de Havillands turned lazily in the air, looped the loop over my turning head, accompanied my swing.

"Entirely at ease"? Was I then not quite carefree, even at Croxley, where I could do as I chose, where there were no standards of behaviour, no necessary response, where nothing was expected of me?

My sister was born in Golders Green while I was at Croxley. Our mother, after a troublesome pregnancy, had a difficult confinement. (When I was born she had known nothing of what to expect: until almost the end she thought her baby would be born through her navel. In consequence the very idea of childbirth was traumatic. Every one of our pregnancies—my sister's and mine—caused her nine months of anguish.)

Soon after her birth the new baby came to Croxley. I remember nothing of being told beforehand or of looking at the baby when she arrived. And yet, of course, I had known all the time, all the long nine months. It is knowing and not-knowing that compounds children's bad feelings.

She was born in August. One late summer afternoon I sat on a log in a pinewood clearing. The pram was nearby. A nurse in a dark green bonnet was reading my favourite book, *Why-why and Tom-Cat*. Why-why, a girl, was forever asking questions, answered by the clever cat. I was Why-why, forever asking questions. But I was also the clever cat who knew all the answers.

I sat on the log, filled with quiet, deep happiness, a release from pain. It was as though the world about me, the warm pinewoods, the resinous smell of freshly cut wood, of trodden pine needles, the baby safe in her pram, had returned, after long estrangement, to a blessed ordinariness.

Later, Mother walked in full sunlight in the kitchen garden, the baby tucked into the crook of her arm, walking between low box hedges, strawberries nested in straw, peapods to be cracked open, potatoes that would come to table small as buttery pigeons' eggs.

Coot was the gardener's name, Coot to rhyme with hoot. He could imitate an owl, curling up his pink tongue through his beard while I sat on his knee in the potting shed. Coot's small eyes twinkled under his cloth cap, his face crinkled with laughter as he curled his tongue, sitting with me on his knee in the potting shed among flower pots stained green, swatches of bast for tying up plants, heaps of compost and sifted soil. Coot's hands were like roots seamed with earthy veins. Sitting on his knee was like sitting in a forked tree. I preferred trees to people, trusting them as my sister was to trust animals. One huge twisted sweet chestnut was my particular friend. From the wood I made forays into neighbouring territory, for every house had its woodland, brought up short when least expecting it by cries of 'Out!' 'Fifteen-thirty!'

Once, during an election campaign, I ventured from the wild into a garden belonging to the local Conservative MP. As a committed Liberal my grandmother did not "call" on Mr Pilditch's wife. Curious to spy out this alien camp I came suddenly, naked, round a clump of rhododendrons, upon a Conservative garden party.

My grandmother gave Liberal tea parties in the dining room. On one occasion she was interestingly agitated over the teacups, draperies falling back over her podgy white forearms, silver chains clinking against the silver teatray. She made tea from a large silver urn on four lion's claws bestriding a methylated spirit flame. Boiling water was directed from a tap into a silver teapot. That day I watched mesmerized as the stream continued to flow, to overflow, to flood the tray, so distracted was she by the talk going on. I remember nothing about the two chief guests except their names: Mrs Pankhurst and her daughter. 'Pankhurst, Pankhurst,' I intoned, shunting round the garden.

Conservatives were not just politically wrong, they were morally bad; they were the enemy. Free Trade was good: its opposite, Protection, was Satanic. The sense that there is a right and a wrong in politics, and that difference, absolute, remains with me. Mr Pilditch got in, as usual.

When a neighbour came in to play Bridge, and Granny was dummy, she laboured up the stairs: 'Nearer my God to Thee', Granny sang to soothe me to sleep, her Indian shawl interwoven with metal thread falling cold on my cheek. 'Now the day is over . . .'

Bedtime was no occasion for sleep but for more intense activity. What I re-enacted was not a play but a regurgitation of what I had heard or read of grown-up life. One game was "Women's Clubs", in which I was rung up and asked to speak in an emergency, crossing London in a taxi, arriving just in time to fill the gap, speak brilliantly and bask in the applause. Another game was "The Land Girl", a musical comedy in which, again, I was called in at the last moment to take over the principal part throughout three detailed acts, with consequent acclaim. One such game would last a whole evening.

I never played games on my own about princes and princesses or any of the fantasies which might have been stimulated by the fairy tales read by my mother. Later I played such games with my sister, I suspect because by then I'd read that this is what other children do. And these true fairy tales took over—I can't, to this day, read *Beauty and the Beast* aloud. I cast myself as the Beast; my sister was always the princess whatever the story. Not till we were grandmothers did she complain that she would rather have been the Beast, and perhaps she would since she preferred animals to people. Or for some other reason. In any case I could not have conceived of myself as a princess.

Grown-ups were what interested me, and for the most part there were only grown-ups at Croxley. I was interested in their false teeth, the food they ate, how it went in, how it came out, what happened in between. Sometimes people came to stay and I was allowed down after dinner for "dessert". After the ladies had retired, trailing long dresses over the tessellated pavement in the hall, I stayed with the men, sitting on my grandfather's knee after he had unlocked a tantalus on the sideboard and brought over a glass decanter of whisky. The talk was grave in tone: I cannot conceive of risqué stories, even of my father's light vintage, at my grandfather's table. They spoke of Asquith and Home Rule; of shares and the Stock Exchange; of golf scores and hazards encountered on the golf course that day, stopping to consider, to tap ash, accurately emphasizing a point, showing stained teeth while replacing a stained ivory cigarette-holder.

I was hot for certainty; and with my grandfather I found it. At the heart of certainty was money, money well earned and well used. Women had no money, and were therefore of little account. Granny had none, had brought none to their marriage. Daddy used to say that the Bennetts were of better family than the Howards; the portraits and miniatures he inherited were from the Bennett side and he knew stories about them all. But this weighed little against the fact that Granny had come to Grandpa empty-handed.

My grandfather supported numerous relatives, as did my father in his turn, including his in-laws. My father hated his father-in-law with a cold hatred. 'He was a hypocrite,' he would say. 'When he was made bankrupt he insisted on paying his creditors in full, beggaring his family to do it. He could have paid them a shilling in the pound.' And in the same breath, veins standing out on his temples, Daddy would add, as though the two traits in his father-in-law's character were connected, 'He was a hypocrite! Went to church every Sunday, had a saintly reputation, yet he never left his wife alone—child after child she had, none of them wanted!'

Money, sex and babies were all jumbled up in my mind. It was Weybridge Granny whom I asked to tell me how babies came out.

'It's like big business,' she answered. And perhaps she really believed this, her mind so closed to her genitalia that she thought of herself as having a cloaca like a bird's.

As to money, and the importance I attached to it in sizing people up, this may well have been a false construction put on what I observed of their behaviour at Croxley. But it was based on a very real impression: the undoubted misery of my mother's parents. At that time financial failure in the middle class meant disgrace, social ruin, the threat of destitution—there was no social services safety net. My mother, with her brother, felt for them with burning humiliation; and I felt this through her. Thence stemmed my uncertainty about "class". My Murray grandmother, in keeping up the front of respectability, worsened matters by acknowledging no obligation, looking on the help she got as her due.

The view of life I got from frequenting grown-ups was confirmed by what I saw on the bottom shelves of my grandfather's library where volumes of *Punch*, from 1887 to 1916, were kept. At first they were picture books. But by the time I was five and could read I learnt about life in its immediacy, not unlike the way a view of life might be received by some beady-eyed child from today's TV soap operas.

From the eighties onwards the cartoons reflected an unchanged world view as seen by Great Britain though, perhaps because they were better done, the Victorian John Bulls, French Mariannes and Russian bears made more impact than Bernard Partridge's crude and savage war cartoons, two-headed vultures dropping blood, babies impaled on bayonets. The cartoons, in any case, didn't interest me. What I pored over were scenes of ordinary life, many of which recalled life in Golders Green, Sheppard's children hopping along to the shops beside pretty young mothers, the sturdy calves of J. H. Dowd's little boys, *contretemps* with Cook in the kitchen, flat jokes which I re-told *ad nauseam*.

The common people were funny as of right, shopkeepers, cockney mothers, taxi drivers. The Tommies were funny too, though sturdy and British. 1916 must have been the worst year of the War; and indeed *Punch* was full of trenches, mud, the odd blood-stained bandage, tins of bully beef, plum and apple jam and Christmas puddings lobbed as ammunition across no-man's land into enemy trenches where bullet-headed Fritz cried '*Ach!*' and '*Gott in Himmel!*' The really bad things the Huns did were reserved for B. Partridge, and then it was the jackbooted, spike-helmeted officers that were the worst. Except "Little Willie", the Kaiser's son, who was just idiotic. And there were the British officers on leave. These gayer scenes tied in with the songs we sang, my favourite being "I'm Gilbert the Filbert, the

Colonel of the Nuts". Nuts wore monocles.

During the war Daddy, exempted from military service on health grounds, worked as a clerk in the Ministry of Munitions. Evangeline and my mother gave concerts in aid of the War Effort and played to wounded soldiers. They took me to a recital at the Alexandra Palace where aliens were interned in considerable discomfort, without, as far as I could see, anywhere to go except this monstrous cold glasshouse. This cannot be true; probably they had sleeping huts outside, within the barbed wire fence. But my impression, got from my mother's compassionate indignation, is that they were unhappy, ill-treated and should never have been there. Among them were many musicians; a string quartet played. Here I have to face up to a curious though widespread aberration on the part of my parents: their double-visioned view of Jews. Necessarily, from my mother's profession, most of her closest friends were Jews. Add to this that after the war my father had a new partner in the business, Cyril Nathan, of whom we were all very fond. Cyril, who had fought in the war, used to come riding on the Heath; he would take my sister up in front of him and canter round the ride with her. We were both a little in love with his dashing, warm-hearted manner and military moustache and later, when I was at school, we kept up a jokey, affectionate correspondence.

For all this, my parents were able to talk of "Them" and of "The Chosen People", a "Certain Race". When Uncle Jim's Glasgow cloth business failed it was "They" who had ruined him. This, I take it, is true splitmindedness, simultaneously holding two incompatible beliefs side by side, yet totally separate. So, early on, I imbibed the beginnings of anti-semitism.

I left the Alexandra Palace thinking they were all musicians, all Jews.

At about the same time, when I was four-and-a-half, my mother took me to Glasgow where we stayed with her eldest, happiest sister, Lena, who married young and had her first child before her own brother was born, early enough to fight in the War and to survive. He must have been about seventeen as I remember him, home on leave in his kilt and boots and puttees thick with trench mud.

In Glasgow Uncle Jim took us to Central Station where a white train painted with a Red Cross came in. We saw stretchers unloaded, bandaged walking cases, blinded soldiers. We followed them to a hospital, Uncle Jim carrying a huge paper carrier of plums for me to distribute in the wards. I remember the bloom on the purple plums.

From the time I could read I believed in the power of words, in the magic of names, of naming to God people whom I fancied had done me an injury. Usually they were doctors. Soon after the end of the war Ferelyth and I contracted ringworm, a disease, I heard my elders say among themselves, spread by 'dirty men in the trenches'. The cure was to have our shaven heads "X-rayed" in Harley Street by Dr Savile, a family friend, but not mine, session after session under crackling, blue-flamed electrified helmets like hair-driers. (For "X-ray" read, more probably, ultra-violet light.) Afterwards the hairs were pulled out with tweezers, one by one, till we were bald. The Harley Street sector, including the dentist and the "oculist", became a place to be dreaded.

Mother had muslin caps made for us, "Dutch caps" they were called. When my sister's hair grew again her fair ringlets had given place to hair as straight and dull as mine.

At the age of five I had my tonsils taken out, like most middle-class children, on the kitchen table by a doctor wearing a wing collar and striped trousers. Working-class children had them nipped or cut out without an anaesthetic in the outpatients' department and were sent home in a bus, vomiting blood into a basin.

'See, it's a pretty lampshade,' said a nurse, putting the pink thing over my face and pouring chloroform over it. Waking, vomiting blood and food, I noted them all standing around, the doctor and two nurses: their names, I told God, were Dr McCall (also a "family friend"), Nurse Nelson and Nurse Sowerby.

That operation was performed in Claygate, not far from Weybridge, whither we had gone to escape the bombing. Zeppelins approached London from the north and east and in 1916, in Golders Green, I was taken out wrapped in blankets to see a slim silver pencil caught in crossed searchlights. Did I actually see it fall in flames over Potters Bar? Often this story was rehearsed, the legendary fireball, how a German had fallen to earth near Pinner, 'so fat he made a hole in the ground'.

So we decamped to Surrey, boxes and baskets and maids, taken to Waterloo Station in a horse-drawn cab with a door at the back.

At Claygate I went to school. I was only there six weeks; but by the time I left, with whooping cough, I could read. I saw at once that there was no point in learning "A,B,C". On the page there was a picture, and below it words, which I recognized *as* words: "The-cat-sat-on-the-mat". On page two: "The-dog-sat-on-a-log". With the picture, and the sound, the words had meaning. My contempt for the alphabet has been a source of trouble ever since, for I have never succeeded in learning it. 'What comes between L and R?' I have to ask myself, confronted with a telephone book.

I loved that dame school. I had two friends, Richard and Clement. We stood under flowering currant bushes, full of meaningful words and the warm scent of currant leaves. In secret they showed me an ivory prayer book with a blob of clear jelly on it.

There were other times of happiness. My bedroom wall was covered with sweet peas, lovelier to me than the flowers outside. My father tied a cushion on the crossbar of his bicycle painted green as a grasshopper, had me safe between his full-stretched arms, making short work of the double weight with his long, strong legs, and rode with me over to Weybridge. He had a key to the back gate of Croxley, an iron gate in a spiked iron fence. We bumped over roots, round trees, among wild daffodils. Now, putting my nose into one of those yellow trumpets, the fresh green-bitter smell is all I need of joy and spring warmth.

Near by, the hard tennis court in a thicket of sweet chestnuts and bracken resounded with cries: Granny was playing tennis with convalescent Australian soldiers in butcher-blue trousers with red ties. She stood in her great bulk, her pin-striped, long-skirted flannel tennis costume, swatting about her with her fishtail-handled racquet. Soldiers sat or lay on the moss-creeping sidelines, variously injured, an arm in a sling, a bandaged head, a crutch laid by. And gas cases with rotting lungs. I had been here before when tennis was in train and soldiers moving about in the wood, in the thickets, the high bushes. My curiosity, unbounded as to what they did, was never satisfied. Some relieved themselves, some coughed up their guts with terrible sounds, some went with the maids who brought out tea. I heard their soft cries, the muted laughter, the retching. But never came upon them, perhaps never dared, or have forgotten.

The war ended while we were in Claygate. The cuckoo took away my baby sister's bottle, I was told: she looked about in the garden for it, crying. And the war ended. An open lorry went down the road with German prisoners standing up in it wearing grey, with round caps, packed like animals, swaying, silent. As with other children "German soldier" was my bogeyman, capable of all bestiality. But these dumb beasts were not soldiers.

'We shall have cream cakes again,' said someone. We went to a village called Claremont with a special bakery to see if they were already celebrating victory.

Coffins began coming up the hill at the road's end, processions of hearses on their way to the churchyard. 'They live in a slum,' a maid told me as we watched. 'They caught the Spanish influenza because they were poor,' she said. Then, sharply, 'If you bite your nails the scissors-man will come and cut your fingers off.'

Not only the poor died. Cousin Howard, whose brother Maurice had been killed in the Flying Corps, died in an army tent. He was seventeen.

We went back to Golders Green.

III
Lessons

WHEN WE CAME back to Golders Green after the war I was six and it was time for lessons to begin. My first teacher was Miss Wells, shared with a tall, pale girl with heavy plaits whose parents were musicians. Miss Wells, who had worked with Miss Beale and Miss Buss, was a retired teacher with methods of her own. She taught us about how the earth went round the sun; she stood in the middle of the room twirling an open umbrella over her head, her once-red hair strained back into a bun, while the tall girl walked round her holding at arm's length a gyrating orange. But I have a literal mind and have never been able to benefit from analogies; I can only see the objects themselves, not what they represent; the umbrella remained an umbrella, the orange an orange. Pictures were better; and words best of all. We went for nature walks over the Heath, tracing the streams from their source, learning what the water contained, learning about iron, observing the iridescent deposit, writing down the word "chalybeate", tasting a fingerful of the stuff itself—not so delicious as Parrish's Food, taken for energy and strength, less like the taste of iron than the latch on the nursery window, sucked for extra strength.

We collected tadpoles in a butterfly net and brought them home in a jam jar. My next-door friend Michael Cullis and I tried cutting off their tails with nail scissors to make them turn quicker into frogs, and must have succeeded in catching at least one or two, for I remember the blood in the water. We felt vaguely guilty; Michael insisted that this was a scientific experiment. Dr Cullis was a scientist, and this became connected in my mind with his fathering so many children. The house became too small for them and they went to live in Wimbledon, so far away that it seemed another world. When

David Braithwaite failed me I had marked down Michael to save me from spinsterhood and the little orphan girl, and his removal was a setback.

Then came arithmetic. Miss Wells brought with her a cube-shaped box containing an assembly of wooden blocks, alternately black and white, which could be piled on top of one another to form a cube. At the bottom were nine "hundreds", flat squares. The tenth hundred was divided into rods, "tens", and one of the tens was subdivided into ten small cubes, "units". The whole cube, of course, represented a thousand. The blocks were beautifully made of elm or boxwood. I held a "hundred" stroking it between the palms of my hands, associating it with the ivory keys of the Bechstein. But I never could connect the blocks with numbers. This began a lifelong fascination with figures, coupled with an unbreachable mental block against the use of arithmetical symbols, ordinary "adding up".

Yet perhaps I retained something of Miss Wells' foundation, some unconscious sense of mathematical values. Presented with a financial scheme, I can sense when something is left out, something wrong. Given largeish sums of money I can almost feel myself weighing them up in either hand, though if I did sums with them the answer might be wrong, noughts and thousands out.

I could not conceptualize, could not take in abstract concepts as quite small children learn to do as part of their normal development. For the same reason my free use of words was affected. My emphasis on *naming* people and things was not a good way of making sense of the world or of seeing how people work. The naming was enough for me. I didn't go on to find out more, to discover what people were really like; it was at best like pinning butterflies into a collection. Words are symbols; and if they are felt to be concrete substitutes for what they represent, lifeless entities, they cannot be used imaginatively, as I was to find when I began to write.

There were exceptions to this limiting view of people as objects. The Hendersons, a Quaker family, were among those who made the suburb their lasting home as opposed to people who waited for an opportunity to leave it. They lived at the top end of our square. Their front door opened upon a smell of rush matting and old books. This was the first time I remember going into a house dominated by books and scholarship; forever after the smell of old, much-read books impregnated with pipe tobacco has been a calming, right-feeling influence.

In years to come, when having to be in Central London was an ordeal, I would make for the London Library, not so much to read as to smell the books, to walk among the shelves recovering my common sense.

In Golders Green the Hendersons' house had the same effect. "In a brown study" is to me at once a state of creative absorption and the Hendersons' house. Mr Henderson's study was brown with calf-backed books, hazy with pipe smoke. Mrs Henderson was brown-skinned, brown-eyed, with a straight, beaky nose, and often wore a brown dress. But the brownness has to do with the pleasure of learning: Mrs Henderson was my first English teacher, though not till I went to the school she helped her sister to run. But before that I sat by her to learn, I don't remember what, only the peace laid on me, the relief of being brought into a state to listen. I sat by her; and painted a twig with scarlet hips growing on it. I sat by her; on the table was a pile of tiny wooden objects, each delicately made, some with handles, a jug, a cup, every one small as a child's finger-nail. The game was called Spillikins, the aim being to withdraw one thing after another without disturbing the rest.

In summer we went through the house into the small garden that smelled of verbena, herbs and lavender. Their garden backed on to a wide strip of grassland belonging to the Water Board, thus protected from being built on, bordered on the far side by a line of Lombardy poplars with their continuous movement of leaves, so that in summer there was always a breeze. A river, I believed, ran under the grass.

When I was six or seven Mrs Edrof Smith came to our house to give us piano lessons, my sister being not more than three or four, yet my recollection is that she shared from the first in the finger exercises which preceded our introduction to the key-board. If this sounds dull, it was not; we played a game called "highstepping horses", singing as we lifted and dropped our fingers on the drawing-room table. With my clumsy, mixed-up lefthandedness, the sense of co-ordination and proper use, enhanced by the sound of the piano when we first repeated our exercises on the keys, was like that of an apprentice learning to use precision tools to make precious things.

Mrs Edrof Smith was rubicund, comfortable and capable, with a bubbling humour that was far from over-serious. Her real name was Mrs Forde Smith, but she preferred her first name spelt backwards, a name which, among other pseudonyms, appeared on numberless graded books, musical primers for generations of children. She it was who wrote "The Jolly Farmer", "Marjorie's on Starlight, I'm on Jack", followed by the familiar "Lullaby" with sustained bass and newly accomplished stretch of sixths.

There is tenderness and loving care in playing an instrument well, as in singing. Like Peter Pan, tenderness is a quality I lack, and prize in others. But in those first finger-movements, accurate and deep-searching, there was the beginning of tenderness.

Mrs Edrof Smith brought us a new music book every week, and my mouth-watering anticipation at the sound of a large crackling brown envelope persists to this day.

Those first piano lessons, together with Mrs Henderson's influence, were an early experience of the satisfaction of work, the surest release from psychic pain. All children suffer, go through periods when life is almost unbearable, partly through circumstances, partly because of their own personality. The fortunate ones are those who, like my sister, know when they are unhappy and can bear the pain. Those who don't and can't are in for trouble later on.

Our life was unusually free for the time. We spent days on the Heath in jerseys and serge bloomers (no shorts then for girls) playing with the Cullises and the Braithwaites. "The Band of Oak Robbers", we called ourselves, playing at highwaymen on an old London horse-bus, at knights and Cavaliers and Roundheads in the watchtowers that bounded the new houses being built below Saint Jude's—the watchtowers had steps and could be used for almost any game. We made a tree-walk along a hedgerow of hawthorn and young oaks, cooling off in summer in a half-dried pond among the reeds, our bottoms on smelly mud, bare toes squelching on bruised mint. No warnings needed, then, about "nasty men", our only enemies the brown-gaitered keepers, there to stop us climbing trees, and what chance had they, in high summer, any more than the Roundheads looking for Charles II in his leafy oak?

Yet, at some time between six and eight, I began to be "not quite like other children". There was trouble at meal-times, always a likely source of tension with my father's food fads, his poisoning fears. Since I took part, it wasn't illogical for me to take the blame for parental disputes. Once, at lunch, Mother cried, 'Between you both you'll be the death of me!' and ran upstairs. There was a terrible thud overhead. I thought her prophecy had instantly come true, and sat on alone at the table, suspended in time, listening to the noises above. Her illnesses terrified me, brought out my ruthlessness. Her infirmities were unforgivable.

There came a time when I was unable to eat between them; could only swallow food in the open air. It was summer. Without demur my mother arranged for me to have a table and chair outside the window and passed the dishes through to where I sat in the trim communal square garden, each standard rose blooming with yellow roses, each rose with its own earwig.

This was only one of several aberrations which must have added to her cares, perplexed as she was between the two of us, adamant in our compulsive avoidances of normal behaviour. I mean that we could not help our eccentricities, bizarre defences against unknown anxieties.

Mother enjoyed shopping in the West End and took me with her. But I began to suffer from attacks of acute anxiety. Women's lavatories, specially, terrified me, the scent of powder partly disguising women's smells, the horror of being shut with her into one of Debenham's mahogany and mosaic cubicles. Not that I could express these fears: I was mute.

I had to be brought home on the top of a bus open to all weathers, soothed with spoonfuls of honey and bathed in a tepid bath infused with Tidman's Sea Salt, as recommended for nerves by a children's specialist. That doctor's name, I noted to tell God, was Hector Cameron. Perhaps it was he who recommended that I should be sent to boarding school.

But before that there was a crisis: I stopped being able to sing. That is to say I developed a break somewhere round A flat and refused to sing above the break. This is of course a common occurrence, I mean the break, and can be worked on. But this I simply could not do. Aunt Evangeline sat in our drawing room listening while Mother gently, patiently persuaded me to try; and try I did. Seeing how painful it was for me, she dropped the idea. I could whistle instead, she said. So I whistled at parties instead of singing. This is the earliest instance of what became a pattern: my failing to fulfil high expectations. And that mostly because of refusing to work hard enough, ducking the rigours of work, which has its pains as well as rewards. Taking into account that my two middle names are "Margaret Evangeline", it may be imagined how grievous a blow my failure to sing was for all three of us.

I should be a writer, said Uncle Sandy, who had this idea all along when he gave me a calf-spined edition of *Alice in Wonderland* and a copy of Alfred Noyes' *Poems*. The idea was that I must be going to be something special.

My mother's sisters sat round the gas fire in her bedroom with their silk petticoats turned back over their great silken knees to get the warmth. She'll do something, something out of the ordinary, there's no doubt of it, they said. It was by way of reassuring my mother. For though I made them laugh I embarrassed them, made them uneasy, an aunt has since told me, staring unsmiling, sizing them up. The trouble was, as I saw it, my being so awfully un-Scotch, so like my father in his "Southern English" ways. English was bad; but Southern English much worse. 'I'm three-quarters Scotch,' I used to equivocate. 'Mummy's quite Scotch, of course. And Daddy's got a Scotch ancestor. He's really English; but he's very ashamed of it.'

IV
The Hall School

I WAS SENT to boarding school just before my eighth birthday, taking with me a trunk full of new clothes, pink and blue striped pyjamas, a pink and blue box of ginger nuts to match, a woolly dog called "Ruff", a birthday cake and my first fountain pen, a slim black "Swan". For the first night these new things were enough, specially the fountain pen which I connected powerfully with the black Bechstein.

Next morning's awakening was into pain so acute, so overwhelming that no other memory remains, not the boarding house nor the dormitory nor the school, nor the children, nor what we ate.

My one idea was to get back to my mother. I leant over some banisters meaning to jump, to break a leg, but lacked courage.

After a day or two I ran away, on impulse, without premeditation. Matron had taken us new girls to watch some dancing in the body of the hall. We sat on the platform. Suddenly I got up and ran, across the platform, down steps to a side door, along a road which turned out to be a cul-de-sac. I squeezed between wall and house on to a dog kennel, ran across the garden with the dog at my heels, climbed two more fences, two more garden strips and ran on till I reached a stretch of heathland where there was cover, never looking back, making for Croxley and my grandmother. Once in the drive I slowed down, certain that she would not make me go back.

But Granny wasn't there. She had gone to London. The maids said they must ring the school; and I sat through an eternity in the Servants' Hall while the gramophone played over and over again, "How we gonna keep 'em down on the farm?"

Matron was coming to fetch me, they said. At the sound of

the taxi I ran into the hall, up the stairs, along the gallery into the billiard room, pushed up a window and stood on the sill as the taxi entered the carriage sweep. I didn't mean to jump, only to threaten. Starched cuffs caught me round the waist.

Back at the boarding house Miss Gillett, the housemistress, took me on her knee. I laid my head against her grey knitted jumper like grey pearl tapioca, and she rocked me, dry-eyed, drained by grief.

I was taken home and didn't return to school that Easter term. But in the summer I went back; and from then on my life at the Hall School took over.

The Hall School, Weybridge, was no ordinary school; it was the creation of a remarkable woman, Eva Gilpin. She had been governess to the family of Michael, later Sir Michael Sadler, and he, recognizing her gifts, encouraged her to start her own school.

The first time I remember her she had come up to see me in bed in the night nursery at Croxley. They were doing a play at school, she told me, called *Aucassin et Nicolette*. They were stuffing cushions to see whether they made a noise. A blue blind flapped. I was eating lemon jelly. I was too young to see the play, but I have only to close my eyes and say the words *Aucassin et Nicolette*, and the blue blind bellies out, I taste lemon jelly and the beginning of something else which is almost a taste on the tongue and at the back of the throat, that promise of discovery, that power to transfix the moment which one came later to associate with her. Moments, memories coloured as much by what was to come as by the past, being as they often were no more than a sudden expansion, a flash from her own mind, caught at, half-understood and then—oh, but years later—coming on the phrase, the painting or more likely some complicated cross-reference suddenly illuminated—'*that* was it!'

Not that her lessons were in any sense improvisations; but one could see her mind working on the prepared material, voyaging through barely charted seas, nearing, standing off, dropping anchor momentarily in some hushed bay of thought (unforgettable then the fierce tenderness of her voice, as though she were finding out the truth of the words for the first time), and off again as if to say, 'There—and there! So much is there for you. But you must get it for yourselves.'

This in time we learnt to do. We discovered how to use a library. We were taken on expeditions and returned with full sketchbooks, paintings "learnt by heart" like poetry, to be described aloud. History and literature, music, French and art were all taught together round a unifying theme, a year at a time, The Jeanne d'Arc year, the eighteenth-century year; and the Oxford year beginning with Saint Frideswide and the kingdom of Mercia and ending with Matthew Arnold and Giles Gilbert Scott. We got the facts, were schooled in the architecture and finally, in a memorable expedition, let loose in the place itself. In some way we were made to feel part of what we learnt: Oxford took separate shape in each of us.

Miss Gilpin was assisted by a small resident staff and visiting staff from London, notably a small mercurial Frenchwoman who had worked with Yvette Guilbert, or studied under her, and who taught us to sing French songs and ballads in the manner of her great teacher. Miss Gilpin taught what most interested her, and as almost everything except maths and geography did she couldn't resist involvement with classes nominally in charge of her assistants, the effect being something like a production team in an experimental theatre, which of course, when we did plays, it virtually was. But between Miss Gilpin and Mlle Honoré there was a special affinity and the sparks they struck off one another lit us up like little squibs and Catherine wheels. As with history and the memorizing of dates, in French Miss Gilpin reserved for herself the hard part, the hammering in of vowels and consonants: between the two women those of us with any degree of "ear" got near-perfect accents.

In art and handwork classes it was the same: influenced by contemporary art she had her vision; and those who saw things differently (Ferelyth was one) met with disfavour. She liked us to cover large areas of paper with clear colours, collages of kettles and jugs reproducing the effects of light, crowds scenes like Lowry's. She disliked small bits of paper; and abhorred Indian ink.

Sir Michael Sadler lent her paintings from his collection of Post-Impressionists. They hung in the school hall above the ribstalls, or on the walls of her history room.

Vivid fragments come to the surface, crossed and re-crossed by later experience. The running red of poppies, the shininess of galoshes, the roundness of a cooking pot, Chardin's wine bottle, Renoir's blue umbrellas at the National Gallery, the name "Crivelli" tasting of jewel colours, Uccello's trampling interlocked armies from which all my battle scenes were derived, a swatch of materials hung over Miss Gilpin's arm, dyed for a school play—magenta, scarlet, onion yellow—the well-known figure, knees flexed, foot in advance, which she cut when she wanted to startle and delight: these are simple memories.

More complex are the recollections of plays, often the result of a year's study, in which we learnt the intellectual and emotional effort demanded of both actor and beholder to sustain an imaginative creation. These plays took place on a bare stage furnished only by a set of steps, a rostrum, I think is the term. The bare-footed, anonymous performers wore short black tunics added to which a scarlet cloak, a sea-green shift might make an effect of brilliance, kingship or water; and moved with a disciplined freedom attained by long practice in Dalcroze methods, a mixture of mime and rhythm, the music measured in counterpoint.

Too young to take part in *Don Quixote*, I remember Criteria high on the steps in a long crimson robe, human windmills gyrating against an imaginary sky, lights moving in a darkness to which Debussy's "Images" gave the reality of a summer night.

As time went on Miss Gilpin's productions, influenced perhaps by Reinhardt, took up more and more of the hall: in *Jeanne d'Arc* Bourgignons tramped from the back of the hall, the English, on the stage, were besieged at Orleans, shouting battle songs with the tears of an army defeated.

The upper forms learnt all the words of these plays, chunks of Froissart, adaptations from medieval French chroniclers, the words, as I remember them, describing Charles's coronation at Rheims . . . "*Il descendit du ciel en forme de Colombe, tenant dedans son bec la Crême Baignée*".

We learnt a great deal of poetry and prose by heart, which

means exactly what it says: words "got by heart" live on, powerful enough to melt even the lump of ice which, as Hans Andersen knew, that heart can become.

As for *The Ancient Mariner*, it remains entire in memory, from the horror of his "fixedness and loneliness' to the relief of "O sleep! it is a gentle thing, beloved from pole to pole!"

And at the end the blessed ordinariness of his return:

> The harbour-bay was clear as glass,
> So smoothly it was strewn!
> And on the bay the moonlight lay,
> And the shadow of the Moon.
> The rock shone bright, the kirk no less,
> That stands above the rock:
> The moonlight steeped in silentness
> The steady weathercock.

We weep, not when things go wrong, but when, against all expectation, they come right.

In *The Ancient Mariner* we plumbed depths of experience which were not then generally allowed to be within the range of children of eleven and twelve. The production, with its inexorable hold upon a nightmare reality, went beyond the bounds of comfortable entertainment. Some parents believed we had been better without it; but none of us would have missed it. We were alive, impassioned creatures capable of an emotional range then, perhaps, as never since, treated as the equals we were, or that Miss Gilpin demanded us to become.

In her genius she chose to play the Mariner one of the most stable, matter-of-fact girls in the school. Most of the action took place on the stage before the Mariner's eyes, isolated on a dark rocklike hulk in the body of the hall, transfixed by his own guilt, ensnared by horrors beyond his understanding, condemned to live through madness and to bear the pains of remorse and recovery—he was an ordinary man, that dark figure, as Coleridge meant him to be.

> In his loneliness and fixedness he yearneth towards the journeying Moon, and the stars that still sojourn, yet still

> move onward; and everywhere the blue sky belongs to them, and is their appointed rest, and their native country and their own natural homes, which they enter unannounced, as lords that are certainly expected and yet there is a silent joy at their arrival.

After the last performance I walked back to the boarding house with Ursula, who had played the Mariner, silent, and sat with her in the empty playroom eating jelly sponge while tears ran slowly down her cheeks. We still said nothing. There was no need; we were true friends.

For I made friends at the Hall School with a naturalness, a reciprocity, a permanence never achieved since.

There were two boarding houses about five minutes' walk from the school, "The Big House" and "The Little House", with long gardens, a pine wood and shrubberies where "the Little Ones" made houses, an orchard, and vegetable gardens. The houses were gas-lit, primitive and smelly in the bootroom and kitchen quarters, but surrounded by long gardens and woodland. In the vegetable garden Miss Gillett and Miss Mattock kept bees yielding a dark honey which diversified our rather brown meals, jam made from dried figs, coarse brown bread. Those parents who could afford it paid for extra eggs and oranges and jars of Keiller's marmalade.

In summer we wore holland overalls that smelled of brown bread, and on Sundays cream tussore dresses and coats. In winter we wore emerald green jerseys and navy kilts that began each term smelling of clean serge but soon gathered chalk and dust from sitting on the floor—there were never enough chairs for Miss Gilpin's history lessons and we arranged ourselves in a horseshoe, sitting up cross-legged, ramrod-straight, bracing our backs by gripping our gym shoes like speckled black fish. Young children's sweat doesn't smell. But serge knickers, not often changed, do; and it is that kilt smell, combined with a whiff of stale urine, which is associated with an ache of concentration, a blessed self-forgetfulness, an almost painful joy—the beginnings of learning to learn.

But this was a gradual process. In the Little House we were tribal, our lives ruled by rituals and portents, specially in the dark, dripping spring term, a time for illness and rumours and story-telling at night in bed with our woolly animals. I scared myself with a story called *The Screaming Skull.* And made a girl called Anna Brooke scream by revealing how rabbits came out of their mothers. She was a sturdy girl from a country home and I can't think it was the information that upset her, more the ghoulish telling of it. Anna kept an orange and black grass snake in her knickers and exhibited it, yard by yard, to the day-boarders during the lunch hour. But that was in the summer term when all was bright and beautiful and plain to see, and we stayed awake late during long hot evenings.

One summer night the bees swarmed in a pear tree in the kitchen garden. We were allowed to get up, and stood among the cabbages and raspberries in our kimonos, pale-green, pink and blue, while Miss Gillett beat on a tin tray and Miss Mattock in her veiled hat climbed the tree and gathered in the bees.

In summer there were frequent thunderstorms, doubly dangerous, it was said, because we were between two rivers: people covered their mirrors with towels and took their wristwatches off. I, alone, was not frightened but filled with an unholy joy, a crackling energy, and this was one more reason to fear, as I sometimes did, that I was mad. Also I did strange wicked things like making everyone in our dormitory pee into our enamel water-jug. In the dormitory a fat white child with some disability stood naked. 'She's a slug,' I cried, 'a fat white slug!' 'Slug, slug!' we echoed, whipping her with the cords from our Jaeger dressing-gowns.

I wanted to rebel, to be against everything, to feel every man's hand against me. This was difficult in a school which, though not a Quaker School, was run by Quakers with a freedom and tolerance in which we flourished, tempered by a discipline we scarcely felt. Quakers are guileful. One autumn term a girl called Melody Kirke determined to start a Brownie pack. Her father was a general. He was a White Russian, it was said, who had fought against Red Russians at Archangel. She was a Big One, tall and masterful, a fallen Archangel herself. She gathered about her the rebels, the "bad girls" among the Little Ones, and drilled us in the playground. Of all aberrations militarism was the most abhorrent to the Society of Friends, and this so soon after the end of the war. Yet we were not prevented. We were offered as our headquarters a large, new, unoccupied chicken house. We sent for handbooks and brown uniforms from Buckingham Palace Road, brass badges, brass-buckled leather belts, Storm Troopers before our time. With two fingers raised in salute we promised to do our best to serve God and the King and to do our duty at all times. (Reading on in the Handbook I doubted I'd ever, at the age of eleven, succeed in becoming a Guide. "Doing your duty at all times", I discovered, included tickling someone's throat with a feather to make them sick when they had swallowed poison. With my pathological fear of vomiting I knew I never could, though in the case of snakebite I could promise to cut a leg with my Scout knife and suck out the poison.)

Melody was old enough to be a Guide and made herself our Brown Owl. We made tracks through the wood, attempted to light a fire by rubbing two sticks together and had lumps of dough at hand to make Australian "dampers". We never lit a fire; but made imitation campfires in the chicken house to sing campfire songs round, including a sad ritual song called "Taps" during which we stood to attention while the British flag, slung over a pine bough, was hauled down at sunset.

Sunset came earlier and earlier. Dank mists hung about the conifers, rain dripped on the chicken house roof. Meanwhile a counter-organization had been started called "Camp Fires". Camp Fire girls wore fringed hessian garments embroidered with Red Indian symbols in coloured wool. Hessian headbands and feathers were worn low on the brow. They called each other names out of "Hiawatha" and were altogether ridiculous and ineffectual. *But* they met in the Grey Room and celebrated their mysteries round a real fire. They were sucking up, we mocked outside the window, they were all "goodies", we cried, hollering Indian cries, hooting like owls in the flower-beds, hoarse from eating beech-mast in the wet kitchen garden.

The Brownies faded away with winter's coming. At night Matron came round with spoonfuls of raw onions and brown sugar, a remedy for our "graveyard" coughs.

Miss Gilpin wouldn't stand for marching unless it was historical. But on League of Nations Day we marched carrying banners and placards, singing "Jerusalem" and led by Lady Layton who, representing one of the leading Liberal families of the country (Sir Walter Layton, among many other activities, controlled the Liberal newspaper, the *News Chronicle*), addressed a large crowd drawn up on a pacific battlefield.

All the Layton family were at school, boys and girls, all ages, all fair and blue-eyed, with faces like seraphic, freshly oven-browned buns.

We were, I suppose, a mixed lot, with a proportion of "unusual" families attracted by the school's reputation, and a fair sprinkling of what I thought of as the "cocoa girls". My early interest in how much money people had was confounded at the Hall School, where the Rowntrees wore scratchy coarse wool stockings instead of smooth black cashmere, and jerseys faded with age darned under the arms. When their father, Arnold Rowntree, came down from York he didn't take them, as other parents did, to the fashionable Oatlands Park Hotel, but hired a back room in a sweet shop on the Green which sold his confectionery.

It wasn't until I was about eleven and caught measles that I began to develop a more normal sense of people as individuals with separate lives of their own rather than as characters with bit parts in a film, recognizable only by attributes assigned to them in accordance with some obscure interest of my own. Ursula Orange stuck because of her name. Elinor Innes was sick in prayers where she stood. A boy spent all his time during the lunch break being an Electric Cow. A day-girl came to a fancy dress party (at which most of us were got up in crêpe paper) as Napoleon's Josephine in a dress of amber velvet. Her name was Laura Dyas. She had creamy freckled skin and piled-up auburn hair. Her father had been killed while hunting in Ireland; she was an heiress, or would be one day. But meanwhile her mother was poor, with worn black kid gloves, and looked like "Dearest" in *Little Lord Fauntleroy*. A romantic story after my own heart; yet I made no special attempt to get to know her.

But when I had measles, friendship came by surprise.

Four of us, Margot, "Wymp", Ursula and I were put in a small comfortable room—the stark noisome "san" over the kitchen being full—to recover. In those days without prophylaxis or antibiotics, epidemics ran unchecked through communities as viruses and bacteria decimated human cells. Illness was dramatic, victims lay like dark battlefields to be fought over. Recovery, on the other hand, was slow, peaceful, no pressure was put on the patient to get well quickly; we drifted back to a gentle consciousness, relaxing as the disease loosed its hold.

Our mothers brought us sponge cakes, jellies, pots of daffodil and hyacinth. As our eyes were affected we could not read but told one another stories and poetry. "Wymp" taught me the whole of "The Lady of Shalott".

And it was during this slow pacific return to life that we formed a lasting bond.

Back in circulation we were inseparable. We thought of ourselves as superior to the rest, and perhaps we were in some pseudo-sophisticated way. We played at being "Stalky and Co". Margot, dark, sallow, with thick expressive eyebrows and a bitter wit, was Stalky. I was a natural for Beetle, short-sighted and a facile versifier, though I didn't then wear "gig lamps" as I should have done, McTurk was unmemorably split between the other two. "Wymp", placid, pretty and rather fat, was the most conventional. I went to tea with her family; the atmosphere was restrained, a little precious. Mrs Wimperis said it was not the thing for women when seated to cross their legs. But "Wymp" must have got away on her own, for she became a painter, asked James and me to supper in her Earls Court bedsitter where we ate cabbage cooked on a gas ring and spread with Shippam's Paste. Of Ursula I shall have more to say.

Margot, the only genuine rebel among us, was a clergyman's daughter. One summer holiday after lunch I got Granny's chauffeur to drive me over to see her. But the great, Victorian vicarage buried in Surrey vegetation was deserted. I peered through the laurels into the dining room. The room looked neglected. The cloth had not been cleared; there were bread-crumbs on it. The cloth, those crumbs, gave me an insight into how other people lived, how differently from us. (Similarly, on another holiday, I called on a boy who was to partner me in a tennis tournament: it was half-past nine in the morning, and I could see through carelessly open doors in the holiday bungalow beds still unmade in untidy rooms. So far from envying the family their liberation I was unpleasantly affected, as when in a train passing the backs of houses a lighted room shows up squalor, steam, washing lines. For an instant I am in that room, it is my life, too dreadful to bear.)

I never told Margot of that visit, feeling that I had spied, exposed what should have been kept private.

With these rare exceptions we never saw one another between terms, wholly absorbed as we were in school life and in each other. What they saw in me I can't tell. I asked Ursula recently whether I had not seemed a disturbed child? Not disturbed, she said, just different from the others.

By the time I left the Hall School, my sister Ferelyth had been there for at least four years. I don't remember her coming, and hardly her being there. This indifference must have laid a chilling hand on her, though perhaps by then she was used to being cut out. It was as good an indication as any of my state of mind, of how, far below the bright, expanding world of active imagination, bits and pieces were kept in blocks as waste nuclear material is said to be stored, frozen at a depth which even the warm contact of friendship could not penetrate.

I came back at the beginning of a term to find I had been put in a single room instead of, as we had hoped, sharing with "Wymp", Ursula and Margot. But, as noted already, Quakers are guileful. My room was labelled "Poet's Corner", a gratifying recognition. A fretwork bookshelf hung over the dressing table, big enough to hold my Collins' Clear-type edition of Dickens, given me by Uncle Sandy on my eleventh birthday. By the time I was twelve I had read through the lot except *Hard Times* which wasn't included. I read under the bedclothes after the gas had been turned down, following the lines by torchlight, licking the batteries to see if they tingled or would soon die, looking for love, not sex but romantic love as in *Little Women*. There is not much love or sex in Dickens, not, at least, in a form I could recognize.

But I did find something of what I was looking for in *David Blaize* by E. F. Benson, a story about love between two schoolboys, steeped in the golden light of an Edwardian summer. How did I come by this book? I can't think of anyone who would have given it me at home; and I certainly never picked it up at school. *David Blaize* came to me out of the blue, a revelation. This, I collected, was how life should be lived. Here I found the love I had looked for in Dickens, and something I was not yet consciously aware of, sexuality. Of the two boys, Frank attracted me more: David was too good. I was aware that they loved each other—at least that Frank loved David with a feeling he was ashamed of. I was much struck by the moment when Frank stood with his kettle looking at David in the bath. Love between men, I concluded, was better than love between men and women, more intensely felt. Love between David and Frank was all mixed up with cricket and classics and poetry which I had come to, idealized, through my father. I kept *David Blaize* to myself.

The friendship between the four of us at school was totally sexless. The semi-sexual, mutually exploratory games I still played in summer holidays when I could find boys to play with were not exactly un-sexy but curious, retarded, loveless. My uninhibited goings-on with grown-up Erskine suggested that more mature sexual feeling can be experienced by a twelve-year-old. But all these activities, conceptual or acted out, were kept boxed away from one another, along with one which contained the idea of marriage as a piece of proper behaviour, desirable but quite beyond me.

I had begun to suffer from unidentifiable little illnesses, mini-breakdowns, a day in bed or the prolongation of an infection, as when symptoms didn't clear up after an attack of gastric influenza. I spent the beginning of the following term at home, tended by Mother, visited daily by a Swedish masseuse, Madame Steinmetz, who administered "high colonic irrigation"—a vaselined tube was passed through the rectum—followed by vigorous Swedish massage. This I enjoyed, not just for the pleasurable sensations but because of the relaxation that followed, the psychological relief. Every day I was washed out, bad wicked feelings washed away, not harshly purged but taken from me. Afterwards I lay in a wicker chair in the garden, fed on bananas and cream.

This is not to say that I was obsessed, as some children are said to be, by a sense of sin. I was quite without insight and led a frenetic external life of hyperactivity; what I struggled with took physical form, lodged in the belly. Nevertheless the ethereal lightness and peace in which I lay after these ministrations, looking at the summer sky and the pale green leafy hedge, were of a Blakeian innocence.

At the Hall School occasional lapses, ill feelings, counted for very little. But at home they caused anxiety on which they fed and grew. After this episode I was taken again to see Dr Hector Cameron the paediatrician. As a result I was to be "kept quiet", not over-stimulated at school. We had begun to work on *The Ancient Mariner.* I was not allowed to take part in the play, a deprivation that aroused Miss Gilpin's tacit but obvious disapproval.

The best cure for these neuroses would have been total absorption in work, in all we were offered at school. And for long periods this was the cure—the last years there were the most fruitful, the best remembered. And of course I laughed and sunned myself in the secure companionship of Ursula, "Wymp" and Margot. We were, I daresay, almost as witty—Margot specially—as we believed.

They were golden days. Times of contentment, walking back with Ursula Watson after the ceremonial term's-end cricket match between Scholars and Fathers, the fathers playing left-handed with a hand tied behind their backs. Mr Watson was a first-class cricketer. We both took the game seriously, oiling our bats with linseed oil. Times of blissful abandonment, riding in Saint George's Hills on Saturdays, plunging down precipitous forest glades after our drunken riding master, ducking under cedar boughs, brought up short, falling over our horses' necks on half-made roads. Times of elated fulfilment, driving back after the Oxford expedition, singing, rushing through evening air under interlaced boughs in our open char-à-banc.

At the end of that summer term, 1927, it was time to say goodbye to "Gilp" (which, to the end, we never called her to her face), sitting in her room with its piles of papers and books with the red "London Library" label, its Victorian furniture, a painting by Signac, all points of light and colour, propped against a wall; she herself sitting in the midst looking at us over her horn-rimmed glasses, her pippin-red cheeks, her leathery voice which seemed always on the edge of surprise. There was a plainness and splendour about her and about her search for truth, for right values, which, however difficult some of us found it to tell truth from falsehood, stayed with us for life.

V
James

I HAD FIRST met James while I was still at the Hall School, in 1926. I was bicycling back from a fishing expedition to a seaside hotel in Bamburgh, carrying a devil-fish in my knickers. He, the youngest, most attractive, least good-looking of three handsome brothers, was getting out of an open, crimson Vauxhall tourer. From then on the tempo of that Northumbrian holiday quickened; for me, life was never to be the same again.

My parents, my sister and I led a life of extreme regularity governed by my father's habitual needs: holidays were planned in January; meals were never five minutes late. The MacGibbons, on the other hand, lived like the lilies of the field. Fatherless, they responded happily to their mother's impulses, which took her anywhere on the spur of the moment. Shortly after their arrival she fell heavily on a rock while bathing and had to be nursed by my mother, thus prolonging their stay and allowing James and me to get to know one another as we might never otherwise have done.

At fourteen he was strong, cheerful, open-hearted and—what was equally important—unusually open-minded. For I, an awkward thirteen, quick-brained, ill-disciplined, febrile, fearful yet avid for experience, would have seemed a very odd fish to a conventional public schoolboy. At once I marked him down; I meant to marry him. This simple certainty filled me with a sense of direction and liberation which gave point to every moment of the day, from those sand-whipped, chittering-bite north-east coast bathes, to wet evenings when the guests at the Victoria Hotel entertained one another. One of James's elder brothers sang "Where my caravan has rested"; a lady recited "Little Tommy's Trousers"; James played the ukulele and sang "Valencia" at the top of his voice. And I, at my mother's behest, gave them my Parisian street cries, learnt at school from Mlle Honoré, a pupil of Yvette Guilbert's. Those raucous, incomprehensible shrieks under the bleak skylight of the games room must have seemed bizarre in the extreme. But not to James, who said later that he had been tremendously impressed. This is what I mean about his open-mindedness.

He used to take their dog out for walks, and it was during these outings that we came to know each other, talking easily, without constraint, a new experience for both of us.

There was an air of easy-going, open-handed prosperity about James that added to his attractions. His two grandfathers had been successful businessmen, one a draper, the other a wholesale whisky merchant, both, as James's elder brother wrote, 'highly respected citizens', ambitious for their children, with due Scottish respect for education. It was traditional that his father, the eldest MacGibbon in the next generation, should go into the Church; and on both sides of the family sons and grandsons tended to become doctors of medicine, naval officers, engineers or civil servants. James never thought about money, or had doubts about class. His father, also called James, had been Minister of Glasgow Cathedral which, in the Church of Scotland, about equals the Archbishop of York. If he had not died in 1922, when James was ten, he would have become Moderator of the General Assembly, the highest office in the Scottish Church.

James remembers him as a man of contrasts. He wore a rimless monocle, not for show, but because only one eye was defective. He was a sparing eater—"MacGibbon lunches" are still remembered by survivors from World War I as a patriotic slogan, an example to all. But he drank a bottle of claret at lunch and another at dinner without any external effect. The Church of Scotland is notable for its plainness and restraint as to vestments, liturgy and ritual. James's father brought ceremony and colour into cathedral services, introducing the mace to be carried in procession, chanted psalms as opposed to "paraphrases" and a general impression of scarlet and purple panoply which, if it delighted some, came near to scandalizing conservatives for whom the Church of England was barely distinguishable from the Church of Rome.

James's parents married when both were in their late thirties. By the time he was born, his mother was in her mid-forties. She was fair, comely, impulsive, with a latent talent for the visual arts, eccentric enough to be unaware of unconventional behaviour, bored by the social demands, the formal entertaining imposed on her. (There is an endearing photograph of James, very small, in a sailor suit, holding the hand of Father Nicholas, Patriarch of the Serbian Church, very tall and long-bearded. 'We shall call the photograph "Old Serbia, Young Scotland"', said the Patriarch when he reluctantly agreed to face the camera.) She made no secret of the fact that her husband's death had come as a release. Remarkably plain-spoken for the time, she conveyed to her sons that they had not been well-suited to each other. From then on the four of them led a peripatetic life, changing houses, holidaying abroad, swanning around in the Vauxhall visiting friends on the spur of the moment.

Seeing James was always a surprise. Surprises were what his mother delighted in. The summer after Bamburgh they drove all night from Edinburgh so that we might discover them at breakfast in our Shap Wells Hotel. The following spring they turned up in London. James and I went about the town in fine April weather. In the dome of Saint Paul's I pretended to be afraid of heights so as to hold his hand. For similar reasons we visited the Chamber of Horrors at Madame Tussaud's, and ended up with a *thé dansant* at Dickins and Jones. He danced well, for like all Scottish boys he had been put through the heel-and-toe routine at a formative age.

But before that, at the end of our Lake District holiday, we had driven over together to Carlisle. He had seen me off on the school train for my first term at Saint Leonard's.

VI
Saint Leonard's

FROM MY ARRIVAL in 1927 to my departure four years later it never crossed my mind but that Saint Leonard's, founded in 1877 to give girls as good an education as boys, was the right and natural place for me to be.

On our first morning the housekeeper took us down to the Supply, next to the school laundry and the gasworks, where we were issued with house shoes, snow boots, belts of webbing and leather for games and calico knicker linings that crackled when we sat down. Our long cloaks, hoods lined with our striped house colours, looked appropriate in the school grounds bounded by the ruined walls and watchtowers of a monastery. We were given corded silk squares in brilliant stripes like those worn by men round their necks with their college or regimental colours. We didn't, though, wear them round our necks but folded like an outsize tie, pinned round our belts on our backsides for easy identification on the playing fields. They were known as "tails". You got a special "house tail" for being in a house team. Those elected few who got into a school team got their "tail" or their "half-tail", the equivalent of a blue or a half-blue. James, who came up to the school with me after we were engaged, said it was a frightful sight to see hundreds of girls bowling as well as boys. But to me it was an inspiring sight to see the broad terraced fields stretching down to the sea filled with fine fluttering silken tails in as many colours as a medieval battle-field.

Without going into amateur Freudian speculation one might ponder over these "tails". For the school had been founded to give us equality with boys, as we sang in our school song:

Here in our halls where our records of glory
Blaze from the boards in their gold-lettered names,
Here in our fields where we tell a new story,
Showing that girls can do something at games.
(*Chorus*) Ad Vitam, Saint Leonard's!

The trouble was that while emulating boys we were not given their freedom. Saint Andrews is set in marvellous country: to the east, cliffs and rocks that Stalky and Co would have made their own. To the west, along with four golf courses, sands curving away to the River Eden, and in the distance the Sidlaw Hills snow-covered in winter. But we were kept playing games. A ramble along the cliffs was a rare treat and never alone but with partners chosen according to ritual. For our Sunday walks and the enforced walks we took when "off play" (menstruating) there was a choice of three, all inland along metalled roads.

Wherever we looked there was beauty, evocative, emotive, tall ruined towers, the nave of the cathedral thrusting out into the "German Ocean", the arched roofless Pends, the scarlet gowns of the University students flying before a north wind along the harbour jetty, our own Queen Mary's Library, a seventeenth-century house, restored with the room where the Queen of Scots had slept and prayed—everywhere a stimulus to our imagination, forever tugging at our hearts and minds. Yet the life we led restricted all communication with what we saw and might have felt, contemplated, taken in. Instead we expended our energy and what must have been presumed to be dangerous thoughts in playing hockey, fives, lacrosse, golf, cricket and tennis—and very enjoyable I found them all. When someone won a scholarship to a university it was announced in prayers. 'Rah! Rah! Rah!' we acclaimed with ritual precision, then rushed back to our houses to change and play games while light lasted, never alone or unoccupied.

As to what I learnt at Saint Leonard's the answer is very little with the exception of plain sewing, a skill almost lost today, and English literature. To my English teacher and to Mrs Henderson at the Hall School I owe what writing I have done since.

Though drama was not a curricular subject, we did occasionally act, often enough for me to discover that this was something I thoroughly enjoyed. I was given a rôle that suited me in a play called *Marigold*: that of a sophisticated French woman who returned to Victorian Edinburgh to ensure the happiness of her deserted daughter. The experience was enough to show me that formal acting (as opposed to our Hall School productions) was something I could do reasonably well. I determined to go to drama school, whether or not I went to university.

There was a Hall School touch about the scenes from *The Tempest* done in the classroom when it was a set book for "O-levels", or "Schools" as these external exams were called. I readily identified with Caliban; and interpreted the part in my own way, playing him as a deformed, unregenerate brute, yet with a frustrated sensibility. When I came to the lines:

> Be not afeard—the isle is full of noises,
> Sounds and sweet airs, that give delight, and hurt not . . .

My brutishness fell away; gradually I stood upright, made whole by the music, transformed while it lasted. I think it still holds good as an interpretation of Caliban. And it was deeply felt: it was how I felt about myself.

My taking in so little of the formal teaching may have been partly because of my place at the back of the class of some thirty girls, short-sighted and probably already a little deaf. Worse disabilities could have been overcome and I truly wished to learn, to apply myself. The point is I didn't mind my place in the back row along with one or two agreeably idle associates. Sustained concentration made me feel slightly ill, and does to this day, though I can't remember being so troubled till I began to grow up. Not ordinary stupidity but a persistent, calculated underachievement dogged me in adolescence and has never been outgrown.

There was one room, remote, high up in the New Building, where calm, order, a dedicated sensuousness were to be found, Miss Kitchin's music room. For the most part she taught only serious pianists with a career in mind. Because of our mother she taught us. (Ferelyth, when she came, wisely distanced herself from the piano and took to the 'cello, an instrument which didn't much interest Mother, though she could be very funny imitating the contortions of lady 'cellists and their knobbly knees.) I had no natural feeling for the piano but Miss Kitchin drew out what musical expression there was and established a technique which made practice an orderly, enjoyable activity. Our one-to-one sessions were a good kind of therapy.

Singing was still my most natural musical outlet. In the school choir that "break" of mine around G flat was of no consequence. I sang "seconds" in a forceful contralto.

Girls are not so self-sufficient and invulnerable as boys suppose. I think of us hurrying through the howling dark in our hooded cloaks to school concerts. Rising on the school platform in our white crêpe-de-chine dresses and shawls and black stockings to sing "Pleasure it is to hear, y-wys, the birdës sing". And "Weep no more". And Betty Snowball, who later played wickets for England and played first violin in the orchestra, bow poised to plunge into that torrid piece, "Dance Number Five" by Granados. "My soul doth magnify the Lord, and my spirit hath rejoiced", we sang, praising the love that we drew in with every breath, that swelled beneath our spencers and our boneless Maidenforms, love which we felt in all parts of our body—love about which we knew almost nothing, but it was all to be given, to be bestowed—oh! to whom?

Love was not allowed in that school. We got an order-mark for stopping to speak to boys, even if they were cousins, on our way down South Street to the golf links. Love was not taken into account there, though some of the teachers, of the generation whose men had been killed in the Great War, were not unloving, albeit in a sublimated form—our splendid English mistress visibly shook in her shapeless cardigan, taking it out on Coleridge, on Milton, on Keats and Wordsworth. Fired by her pure gem-like flame, we shared her love to our lasting benefit.

If two girls got fond of each other they were separated, literally separated, for in my house every girl had to take another girl to be her "walking-over" partner, that is, to be inseparable except during school hours, no doubt for convenience, to keep tabs on one another, for there was always a place you had to be in at the right time. To make matters worse we were layered in years, and these pairs had to be in the same year, which narrowed the choice. It was not likely that many would get noticeably fond of one another in these forced marriages of convenience but if they did they were made to change partners.

Some girls got on well enough, as couples shake down in marriage. But at the beginning of every term there were always those who smelt or had dandruff or who came from Tierra del Fuego, as one pale withdrawn child did, and the cussed ones. The worst disgrace was to be unpartnered, to be compelled to "tack on", making an unwelcome threesome. In the Lower Fifth and the Fifth I waited every term for new girls to arrive, they came up to be seized one by one like Captain Hook's captives out of the hollow tree. But none of them lasted.

A girl I had known at the Hall School arrived a year later than me; being younger but cleverer she was put straight into the Fifth and she was the one girl with whom, but for this inhuman law, I might have made some workable accommodation. She was Laura Dyas who at the Hall School fancy dress party had come dressed in amber velvet as Napoleon's Josephine. Within a week or two I felt trapped. Fifteen, sixteen are awkward ages for the most normal adolescents; but I couldn't have withstood close proximity to anyone, just as later, for many years, I could not tolerate being left alone in the room with any one person, least of all my mother—anyone who cared for me, wanted to help. Laura, I think, wanted to help, though in what way is impossible to define; I wasn't conscious, myself, of need. She stuck, I forget for how many terms, enduring what she afterwards spoke of as cruelty, of which I was oblivious.

Far from being a self-styled rebel, as at the Hall School, I cared for nothing but to be like everyone else, taking as my models types who were adequately clever and naturally conventional. Laura stood out: she was quite hopelessly, undisguisedly unlike anyone else, too strikingly distinguished with her creamy skin dusted with nutmeg freckles, too Irish, and with far too much curly coppery hair, hitherto worn loosely tied, which our housekeeper vainly tried to subdue, twisting it into plaits, flexing her muscular forearms as washerwomen used to wring sheets.

'She has too much *character*,' pronounced one of my models of normality, biting off the word "character" like a pretty cat biting off a mouse's head.

My break with Laura occurred in a curious, unlooked-for way: I was taken up by an older girl, House Captain and Secretary of the School Literary Society. I was leaning out of the schoolroom window looking at the last of the cold spring twilight over the sea when she joined me, putting an arm round my waist. She was trembling. Of all the strange encounters of my life this is still the least explicable: nothing had prepared me for it. She was unattractive and I had never liked her; she had bullied us when we were younger at games practice; she was beefy and red-faced and played lacrosse wearing one black kid glove which somehow looked common.

Yet here she was with an arm round my waist, trembling. I had never seen an arm round anyone's waist at Saint Leonard's. I had not trembled myself since, at the end of my first term's long homeward journey, I had sunk down on my mother's knee, at fourteen almost bigger than she was, and was warmed back to life. After that the transition between home and school had got easier and easier till all feeling was modified to cold custom.

Now, with this older girl, I too trembled, filled with a growing warmth. Nor was the wonder lost on me of the privilege conferred, of her being House Captain and Secretary of the School Literary Society.

She asked me to "walk over" and no doubt I ditched Laura. We used to sit in the potting shed, hugging one another and trembling. I sat on her knee. This was all we did; and we never spoke of it. We knew we were doing wrong; but I felt transfigured. Because of her position, I suppose, we were not suspected, as in Soviet Russia a member of the Politburo might get away with worse than murder.

Our short association ended after she came to stay during the spring holidays. At home and when we went out dancing with "the boys", as by now we knew James and his brothers well enough to call them, she simply did not do. The glory fell away. And the next term I refused to "walk over", even though this meant that I had to "tack on" to one couple or another, the ultimate disgrace. In summer the house team had cricket practice after supper. In that northern twilight which never quite gave way to darkness we stood in a circle round the House Captain who hit cricket balls at us at close range. In this way she had her revenge, putting the full force of her stocky frame behind her bat. I was to play in the school concert and my fingers were like sausages.

But I owe her what outweighs all other considerations: she enlarged my reading which, for too long, had been undemanding. On Sundays after lunch there was a period called "stale" when we were made to read "classics", including D. K. Broster and John Galsworthy whose novels I read for the same reason as, long ago, I had licked through Dickens, and with more of what I sought. Now I got on to Jane Austen and Virginia Woolf. *Orlando* I read on the train journey between Saint Andrews and King's Cross. And in the Hospice where I had been sent for a few days' quiet before exams, lying in the garden on my tummy I read *Anna Karenina*, skipping Levin's political economy. Here at last was the love I had looked for in manifold form, passion larger, finer and more tragic than I could have conceived.

Except for the extreme cold I should have said, if asked, that I had been thoroughly happy at Saint Leonard's. Even our incessant hunger had something bracing about it; wanting to eat all the time made me feel strong, healthy and normal. There was a price to be paid for achieving this dicey equilibrium. Part of what got battened down was any serious attempt to discover, pursue and work, however painfully, at my true bent. Typically, after working out of school hours on a paper for the Lit. Soc. about Robert Louis Stevenson, I scrapped it at the last moment for an amusing little squib on Daisy Ashford's *The Young Visiters*. This divergence is not to be blamed on the school which, after all, was there to be used, but on what amounts to a pathological dishonesty. Those nonconformists, among them Laura and my sister, who knew what they *didn't* like about the place, got on better, stayed more or less sane.

I may have been unable to profit academically from Saint Leonard's, but in another way the school had a lasting effect. I continued to walk and talk as I had learnt to do there, with an added uneasy arrogance, a note of false assurance of my own.

To this day in a tight corner, in shops, hospitals, in an unfamiliar environment, conversing at a party with a Service wife, opening the door unexpectedly to the Vicar, a brisk, high heartiness springs up unbidden, all the more disconcerting for being in such sudden contrast to my usual somewhat dour expression.

Before my time, without in the least knowing why, I gave up, decided to leave. I had had enough.

Towards the end of the summer term when we were doing our School Certificate exams, a letter came from Mother. She had been taken ill and was to undergo an emergency operation. She seemed as though she might die; it was a farewell letter. I crossed the hall where we were assembled for prayers, looking for Ferelyth.

It was Speech Day. In the school concert I played, not the modern piece originally chosen for me but one I had heard my mother play, Schumann's "Romance" in F sharp major. For once I played well. And she was not there to hear me.

That afternoon I went up to the platform to be given the Pelham Pearson Prize for original verse.

As for School Cert, I failed in botany, thus, since I had only taken the minimum five subjects, failing altogether.

At the beginning of the Christmas term, my last, I was sent for to see the headmistress. My previous interview with her had been in 1927 during my first term, an occasion of nervous awe for normal new girls. But, fresh from Miss Gilpin, I had passed through the outer office into the inner sanctum with nothing but happy anticipation. When asked what I wanted to do when I left I had answered cheerfully, 'I'd like to be a Member of Parliament and a writer. Oh, and an actress if there's time.'

This had all seemed possible, not too tall an order. If she thought so she didn't show surprise, only a warm, toothy smile. She was an Irishwoman of gentle persuasive charm, as I later observed standing near her on the platform in the choir.

At my second interview she looked grave. They were all, she said, distressed at my decision to leave. I was one of the girls who had been expected to go to Oxford. As to failing my exams—was it perhaps on account of my mother's illness?—I could take them again. Was there any other reason? I couldn't have told her; there was no good reason. I had had enough. Using my mother's illness as a pretext I said I wanted to be near her, to look after her.

Look after her! I had been to see her soon after her operation in some turretted "nursing home" at the top of Fitzjohn's Avenue, lethally ill-adapted for major surgery. Even I could see that she was uncared-for. Half-joking she said she looked like the Union Jack, tracing with her finger a line from her breastbone downwards and another across.

'I must get out of here,' she whispered as I held her hand, standing by the bed terrified, poised for flight.

'But you've only just had your operation.'

'I must get out of here,' she repeated, and I saw she was afraid.

'Don't go,' she whispered.

Sickened by her fear, I withdrew my hand and left the room.

Towards the end of my life now, I have come to believe that there is no absolution for acts of cruelty, whatever the motive. They were done, they exist, to be borne, to be lived with.

Some ten days later she came home unannounced, alone in a taxi, bent double, crawling almost, up the garden path and into her bed. Thereafter, under her direction, Bessie the cook changed her dressings.

VII
Breathing Space

After a series of furnished houses, my parents had settled in a house in Hampstead, a compromise between my father's need to be near a golf course and my mother's wish to be within reach of the West End in a place as unlike Golders Green as possible. Here I idled away my days in contentment. Perhaps after the rigours of Saint Leonard's I needed a break. Every morning for a while I ran down Fitzjohn's Avenue wearing a patent rubber reducing corset (from being too thin I now felt too fat), to Belsize Park where a friend of my mother's gave me singing lessons, followed by a tutorial in Middle English by the singer's daughter's bearded boy-friend—the nearest I ever got to the idea of going to Oxford.

There followed a spell in Paris with an elderly lady who looked like the elephants' friend in the Babar books, and lived in just such a corner apartment. I practised the piano four hours a day and had lessons from a teacher who taught me a new method of working in thirds, sixths, octaves and chromatics, using the thumbs on black notes, which might have been useful had I not given up practising altogether once back in Hampstead.

I continued to write in an aimless fashion, filling a notebook with random observations, scraps of dialogue overheard on a bus, descriptions of the countryside near north London, where we drove out for picnic teas, based on Galsworthy's elegiac pieces in *The Inn Of Tranquillity*. And had the gall to take my efforts round to Lady Rhondda, editor of *Time and Tide*, who lived next door and was tolerant enough to comment that I might, just possibly, become a writer. I had no idea, then nor for many years, of what this meant, the pain, the persistence, the moral and physical strength needed. Writing was seen as a kind of magic: reading a novel or a short story, I did not stop to learn how it was done. And this myopic reluctance or inability to *look* at the shape or substance of a piece of work—my own or anyone else's—was linked with a worse defect: my lack of insight, limiting insight into the lives of others. I was curious, I "observed" them but was insensitive as to what they might be feeling.

An example is my visit to John Galsworthy. I had written to him while I was in Paris telling him what it was that I admired about his books. My letter, he replied, was the kind authors most like getting. Our correspondence continued. When I was back in Hampstead, finding he lived near by, I asked myself to tea.

'Ah,' he wrote back, 'that way disillusion lies!'

I went, all the same, wearing a suit that has never been supplanted in my affections—one gets as fond of clothes as of friends. It was in tweed the colour of grass in early spring with astrakhan revers the colour of a brown spaniel, and a bowler hat to match with a small green and scarlet bird over one eye. Our tea-party was a tête-à-tête—his wife, he apologized, was lying down, they had just crossed over from Paris (Ah, I thought, Irene!). He offered me a scone.

Mr Galsworthy had been right. We had nothing to exchange. He asked me early on if I liked dogs? I didn't; and my pretence was hollow. He looked grave, fine-featured like his photographs, but was not forthcoming. After a polite interval he asked if I would excuse him, he ought to go up and see his wife. I wondered if he had liked my hat. From time to time he had given it a fixed stare, then looked away. Perhaps, I thought, he had been sick in the Channel.

How long did it take me to work out that above all things, even above cruelty to women, he hated cruelty to animals? No doubt it was in his mind that astrakhan was stripped from live lambs. I could have told him the bird wasn't a real bird.

I had begun to entertain ideas of involvement, of romance, of marriage, but remotely, enislanded in Frognal like the Lady of Shalott. The trouble was, of course, meeting boys.

James had quite gone off, being a debs' delight in Virginia Water by night, working for a publisher by day. Everything seems to have happened to James by chance. Constant Huntington, who ran the London office of Putnam—another firm in which my grandfather had "an interest"—shared a car with my father at my grandfather's funeral, and on the way to the Golders Green crematorium they passed James standing on the pavement, hat in hand, paying respect to the cortège as is customary in Scotland.

'I should like to have that young man to work for me,' said Constant.

'I should think you could,' replied my father, 'he's seventeen, wants to leave school, and his mother's thinking of putting him into the motor trade.'

And though James sometimes regretted not staying on at his philistine Scottish public school and following his brother Rab to Oxford, he had a head start over his publishing contemporaries, an advantage in the early thirties when unemployment was high. And his employer saw to it that he had a thorough grounding in every aspect of his trade, an advantage lost today when, in one of the enormous organizations which publishers have mostly become, a man or woman can find themselves stuck in "marketing" or production for life, and never see a book through from its inception to publication day.

What with the Surrey girls, mixed foursomes and ballroom delights in season on the one hand, and Constant Huntington's literary world on the other, it's not surprising that James was off rooting in fresh woods. When we were both eighteen (we are the same age for two months in every year) he asked me to a golf club dance. I wore my new ivory satin Vionnet model dress; being cut on the bias it fitted perfectly without fastenings, slipping into it was like having cream poured over your head. James fastened the clasp of my cultured pearls, standing on the chilly landing of his mother's house before dinner. But it was no use: he thought me a pretentious intellectual snob. I thought him a bourgeois bore.

Yet we never quite lost touch. He stayed in my mind, a stable figure among the shadowy, bizarre fantasies of a prolonged adolescence.

Of those families we knew I liked best the Annans. Fanny Annan, my mother's friend, was half American, half French, and perhaps her American side contributed to her wide smile and her outgoing friendship. She was the most elegant woman I had ever seen. With her fine bone structure, her skin like porcelain, her hair *en marquise*, she reminded me of an 18th-century French painting. And she had the practical outlook of a French housewife. Having been up to see Noël and Tom at school I could see why it was said that their mother, repelled by the domestic uncouthness of Winchester, had turned it down in favour of Stowe. What finished her, apart from the cold and the plumbing, was the idea of boys at breakfast throwing stone jars of marmalade from one to another.

In my search for happy families—I was always on the look out to see how other families behaved—the Annans rated high. My impression was that they were not conspicuously what my family would have called "well off" but that they made the most of what they had, and that their house in Gloucester Terrace was often full of their children's friends. I looked forward to visiting them, to the charade parties, the amateur theatricals. Later we came to know Noël, now Lord Annan, well. James published his book, *Leslie Stephen*, a classic precursor to Quentin Bell's life of Virginia Woolf, soon to be re-issued in a revised edition. But in these early days his elder brother Tom was my friend. His attachment gave me encouragement—that part of me which, from years past, still dreaded spinsterhood and "bringing up a little orphan girl as mine". He made me feel that I could be attractive. On leaving school I had bought a second-hand open Morris, outwardly spry but, like a horsecoper's cheat, full of dangerous hidden faults. Tom showed his devotion by stripping her down with me on Sundays. She frequently blew her gasket and we spent hours with spanners detaching her filthy cylinder-head and tucking her vital parts under what looked like a small electric blanket. Then away down the Barnet by-pass at top speed only to conk again before we reached The Spider's Web. These roadhouses on the new by-pass roads were semi-rural nightspots easily reached from town and much talked about with their all-night licences and heated swimming pools. The nearest I ever got to one was being driven by David Braithwaite down to Great Fosters near Egham, an impeccably respectable haunt, to dance and dine. (I do love *dîners-dansants*, each intermittent course getting thoroughly shaken down.)

Tom asked me to a dance near a house his family had taken in Graham Greene country near Berkhamsted. After it was over we all got ready for bed and lay on the hearthrug round the fire drinking cocoa, I in my new fashionable all-in-one satin pyjamas with coffee-coloured appliqué lace round the wide hems.

Noël introduced me to the new kind of singing called "crooning" and took me to hear Bing Crosby, of whom he spoke with reverence. I've forgotten the film. There were quite a lot of us there—it was the kind of outing I could never have had otherwise.

These conventional, agreeable contacts were cut across by a strange figure, Vittorio Orsini, a cowboy from Idaho whose real name was Victor Baer. He had been turned into an Italian tenor by a Howard relative, an American expatriate living in Fiesole.

He visited us often for my mother worked with him and accompanied him when he got engagements. The best of these was at the Coliseum when Gracie Fields was top of the bill. James and I and the rest of the family had the Royal box. It was cup-tie night. The cup had been won by a Lancashire team and Gracie sang encore after encore, flawlessly, from top to bottom of her enormous range, till her hair fell down over her face and every one of us was transported to heaven, in ecstasy though not in hysteria—a post-war phenomenon. Gracie, Mother told us, was just as adorable off-stage as on, so that she and Victor and everyone else shared in her glory.

I was bowled over by Victor, not so much by his physical attributes as by what he taught me. I have always been a sucker for people who tell me things, who instruct me as he did, going round the picture galleries in his funny fur coat, tossing his wavy hair back as, with finger and thumb extended, he showed me how this or that Italian master used paint. Ostensibly, and perhaps in truth, he loved my mother; but my dad, who supposedly didn't take an interest in his children, said, 'What's that fellow up to? I'd watch out for him.' Mother laughed and thought his suggestion ridiculous: all Victor did was to take me out to the cinema, or I would drive him in the Morris, in deep winter, to Berkhamsted Common where we sat under his cloak and he cooked Horlicks on a Primus; we ate dates and he described how he went "on the Bummel" in Germany down the banks of the River Main and how he would take me if I came to Frankfurt in the spring. All this I told her. But there was a bit more to it than that. At night, in the Devil's Punchbowl at Hindhead, he went down on one knee and I sat on the other while he sang Strauss's "Zueignung". He cooked spaghetti Bolognese in his flat and afterwards we lay pressed together on his divan, he with his slate-blue eyelids tightly shut, in a delicious but perhaps for him painful agony. Believing that my navel was my organ of reproduction I supposed that safety lay in keeping on my suspender belt; but probably I was in no danger of losing my maidenhead and Mother may have sensed this, so that both she and Daddy were right up to a point.

In spite of reading about sexual reproduction in a Victorian medical book for laymen taken from Granny's bookshelf and surprisingly informative—how fascinated, how baffled I was by the reference to "a sac of goldbeater's skin" in the birth control section—I had only the most general notions on the subject. Later in Africa on safari in a boxbody in the Rift Valley, looking for lion with one of Aunt Soph's cousins, lying alongside him with nothing between us and the stars but a swinging great bunch of bananas, I told him about Victor and wondered if he had perhaps been impotent. 'Don't you know?' he asked, hugging me as tightly as he could through layers of blanket and sleeping bag. Even then I was not quite sure: in Aunt Soph's cousin's case it could, I thought, have been his pipe.

It was to ease my unfulfilled passion for Victor that I was sent to East Africa. I had planned to follow him to Frankfurt, ostensibly to live with a family, actually to live with Victor. About this time James had been given leave from his publishing job to complete his education and learn German. Shortly before he left for Berlin he asked me to go to the theatre, and I called for him at Grosvenor House where his peripatetic mother had taken a flat. Walking towards Piccadilly I remarked how sad it was that hansoms had become such a rarity, how much I would have liked to go in one. Instantly a hansom appeared: this sort of thing frequently happens with James. As we clopped along Piccadilly he got out his pipe, and all the way I could see his profile against the lights, as he patted and tamped it. By the time we reached the Criterion I knew I was on the wrong tack with Victor. James went off to Berlin. But I stayed at home, nursing my hopeless passion for Victor till I was sent to Mombasa to get over it.

VIII
Africa

WITHOUT A QUALM I waved my parents away at Tilbury and settled down to unpack my tropical outfit—dresses cut away under the arms to let out the sweat, tussore suit for journeys up-country, a terai, or double felt hat, against the tropical sun. As I came on deck the ship lifted under my feet, lights faded along the low Kentish shore, ahead a lighthouse blinked. We were at sea! Never having drunk anything stronger than Barsac, I turned into the deserted bar, determined to sample a different drink every evening.

'A John Collins,' I said, looking down the list. In the same spirit I sampled everything the voyage had to offer.

As we approached Mombasa, after days of salty sea air, the warm breath of Africa came to us across the waters.

My uncle's house was on the highest, airiest part of the island, the walls folded back, turning the building into a playing-card house. As I descended the stairs that first evening, there, drawn up like a musical comedy chorus, all white monkey jackets and Brylcreem, were the boys of the Union Castle Line. From then on I led an entirely open-air life.

Waking at dawn on my verandah, I drove through silk-soft air to bathe in a cove which, on this coral island, had been made sharkproof. After a breakfast of coffee and paw-paw with a squeeze of fresh lemon juice, it was my pleasant duty to drive my uncle to his office along avenues of scarlet flamboyants, past the "native" quarter through a pale brownish haze smelling of burning camel dung and spices. Uncle Mat had a chauffeur; but such small duties were laid down for me, as when before lunch I mixed their pink gins and bitters—'A clean drink', as Aunt Grizel never failed to remark. In these small ways, their own daughter being grown-up and married, they bound me to them and their way of life.

In the heat of the morning Aunt Grizel and I drove out paying calls, or received friends at home. Though she had a telephone, my aunt often used a houseboy to carry messages from one house to another. The message was called a "chit", held aloft in a cleft stick by the running boy in his long white gown caught up between the legs. Her servants spoke a kind of pidgin English called "ki-Swahili", which, I felt, was somehow rather for my aunt's benefit than theirs. "Leti chai, boy", I learnt to say, ("bring tea"). And "Maji mazuri, boy" ("fresh water").

The house I liked best, though it was in a hotter part of the island, belonged to the Hanbury-Brownes, he being an important Government official, a Provincial Commissioner. It was a lovely seventeenth-century Portuguese house walled like a fortress, with purple and magenta bougainvillaea spilling over down to the water. Up that channel Arab dhows sailed with carpets from Asia after crossing the Indian Ocean, waiting for the monsoon, waiting for a full moon, drumming, thankful to be safe home. My aunt despised the Hanbury-Brownes rather, for seeming to be hard up, for their faded chintz covers, their thin worn Georgian silver. There was nothing personal in this, just that they should have made more of a show as representatives of the Crown.

I sat on a black satin pouffe eating scones, drinking tea that sweated out under the knees as soon as swallowed. Aunt Grizel took me to task: 'You talk too much,' she said, puzzled, mortified, 'either you talk too much or you don't talk at all.' She was formidable, my aunt, large, well-corsetted, her stern features striated like weather-worn limestone under a fringe like lace-bobbins that shook when she was agitated. She was as unlike her sister, my mother, as could be. Between her and uncle Mat, small, bald, brown-eyed, whom I grew fond of and wanted to please for his own sake, I learnt what was expected of me within the framework of their Victorian-Scottish standards. Through their eyes I saw something of the awkward, uncertain arrogance which spoiled their wish to take pride in me, their niece, among their friends.

My afternoons were my own. While they slept I read under my mosquito net. I had brought a trunkful of books with me, novels picked at random from Hachette's, multi-volume sagas, one about a French Catholic wool family in Northern Fance, another about a Protestant cognac family in the South-West; and one whose fifteen volumes seemed to be set in and around the *Gare du Nord.* Also I read Paul Valéry's poetry, Galsworthy's plays and *Marius The Epicurean* by Walter Pater. The incongruity between this cultural mishmash and my surroundings never struck me. It never occurred to me to read about the present, about Africa.

Instead I wrote long diary-letters home. And exchanged letters with James. Constant Huntington had introduced him to a Berlin family who satisfied his idea of what was suitable. Frau von Nostitz was Hindenburg's niece, and kept open house for writers, musicians, painters; she saw to it that James got full value for his money. He soon became her escort—they were constantly 'making expeditions. Embassy parties, concerts, exhibitions, Communist Party meetings in the Alexanderplatz. Introductions to the ex-Crown Princess of Germany or to Furtwängler are of no more consequence than meeting prominent communists'. He walked round the Wannsee having long talks with Renata, the fourteen-year-old daughter of the house. He had bicycled through the Hanseatic towns almost without stopping and felt "awfully done up". Working by day for a printer, he hardly ever went to bed before three,'clocking in at seven a.m., bicycling home in time for a bath and tea before going out for the evening. Berlin winters can be as cold as Moscow, it's the intense cold, I think, that keeps me awake, one can do with little sound sleep'. He and Frau von N. toured Germany, staying with her relatives in castles. He taught Count Freddie Münster to tap-dance. They took a taxi from Magdeburg to Berlin, he ran out of money, had a "cuckoo-label" pinned on all his possessions showing that they belonged to the State.

More and more frequently he wrote about the Bauhaus.

In reply I described moonlight picnics, rugger played in the soft sand with a girl as a ball, dancing almost every night, dinghy sailing with a Union Castle boy called "Chappie". I had had white ducks made to my own design by an Indian tailor who chewed betel-nut as he measured my crutch, spitting out the crimson juice. Everything about Africa was extravagant, oranges as big as grapefruit, cashew nuts hanging like little crescent moons from fruits as beautiful and poisonous as the apple in the Garden of Eden.

Every afternoon punctually at four a breeze sprang up to suit the British who rose from their beds to play games ("Leti ball, boy"). At six the breeze dropped, leaving us in thick tropical darkness as, bathed and changed, we sat with our drinks and sundowners.

At the cinema the Indians were segregated with the "natives", who, in those far-off days, were never called Africans. I wondered what they made of Jeannette MacDonald, Nelson Eddy and Maurice Chevalier in their sky-blue and gold uniforms, and the martial, marital music that accompanied those Hollywood spectaculars which were our constant fare.

Dining out with my uncle and aunt, strict precedence was observed, the Hanbury-Brownes leading, followed by my aunt and uncle and then the Sanitary Inspector and his wife. This protocol was maintained when queuing up for the lavatory—if there was none, as in one old-fashioned building, a chamber pot placed on a chair was emptied in between.

On 25 January, Burns' Nicht (and my birthday and Jeanne d'Arc's), the large Scottish contingent gathered at our house, kilted, monkey-jacketed, tartan-sashed. The menu ran more or less as follows:

> Wee crimson-tipped scrappits [hors d'oeuvres]
> Ayrshire neeps, Moithered tatties . . . etc.

Whisky was drunk, faces sweated, darkened, seemed to swell in the candlelight as, with the cranking of a gramophone handle in the hall, pipe music sounded, as wild and sad as ever in the Scottish highlands. Talk was hushed. Now entered the tall Head Boy, white-robed with scarlet cummerbund, on his head a platter bearing the Haggis as he glided in ritual dance round the table. Toasts were drunk, spoons and forks plunged in the steaming paunch.

When all was eaten there was the final toast. My uncle rose to recite:

From the lone shieling of the misty island
Mountains divide us, and the waste of seas—
Yet still the blood is strong, the heart is Highland,
And we in dreams behold the Hebrides!

(These lines, of course, are by Walter Scott. Nevertheless my uncle always quoted them on Burns Nicht.)

My aunt took me up-country. The journey to Nairobi lasted two days. Can it be true, as I remember, that the train was halted while she and I drove through the jungle to dine with a District Commissioner and his wife? Certainly I was made aware of the importance of being a Union Castle Line representative in a country where, it was said, the transport of people and freight brought the surest financial reward. And I saw the respect and affection in which my aunt was held, for all her tight-reined ferocity of manner. This young couple had been married from my uncle's house, as was often the custom when girls came out from England. The bridal suite was kept in readiness.

During our tour we were rarely below six thousand feet above sea level so that, while the nights were freezing, the days were burning hot; and this, with the immense scale, the contrasts, the intemperate splendours of the Kenyan landscape, kept me in a perpetual state of exhilaration and wide-awake hunger.

I was most hungry in Limuru, a town on a windswept plain nine thousand feet up. Staying with the manager of the Standard Bank we sat on till long after the dinner hour: we were waiting for Captain Fairfax-Lucy. At last he entered, a commanding figure—he could, I thought, have been Andrew Marvell's Lord Fairfax himself. He apologized for the delay—he had had to kill a boa-constrictor hanging in the path of his car. We waited on till he had bathed and changed into evening clothes.

At the Kakamega goldfields I was given a Kruschen bottle full of gold dust. The goldfields couldn't be extended, my aunt said, because they would have run under "a native reserve". An example, she said, of how the development of the country was held back by Government policy. The white settlers were continuously at odds with the civil servants whose mandate was to protect "the natives" from exploitation, to hold the land in trust for them till they grew up sufficiently to manage it for themselves. 'They will never grow up,' my aunt cried, 'they are perpetual children, their brains are smaller than ours!'

These "natives" were sometimes distinguished by tribal names, as when we visited the Masai, favoured by my aunt who felt safe with them, for they were fine fellows in their own primitive way, hunters, lived on blood and milk, proud but never uppity as, for example, the Kikuyu tended to be. They put on an *N'goma* for us, a tribal dance, during which I glimpsed my first adult penis, only one, and that surely by mistake? In exchange for a cracked mirror I took away a Masai belt and a short *panga*—a sword—sheathed in leather embroidered with pearl buttons. The reddish leather smelt of dried blood, sweat and cow dung. When I got home I sometimes lay on my bed with closed eyes, breathing in and out, preserving that smell of Africa.

Though there was no easy occasion for white women, at least visitors, to meet Africans I was allowed, while visiting Aunt Soph's cousin—he who hugged me through our sleeping bags on safari in the Rift Valley—to walk on my own about his coffee shamba with, as a precaution, a small flat automatic in a leather holster. This was because a neighbour had recently been clubbed to death while canoeing on his lake. Were the murderers found, I asked, were they known? Possibly, my cousin replied, probably they were known to the police, but the man had treated his workers so cruelly they were not prosecuted. Since I could not speak their language I found it difficult to make friends with the women and children outside their round huts. Ignoring me, the women continued to pound their mealies, carry burdens on their heads in the way that television has accustomed us to seeing, but which then disheartened me as I put myself in their place, imagining the monotonous hardship. The children, with flies clustered round their eyes, ran away at my approach. Lying on the ground in the dust a woman was giving birth, surrounded by women chanting, clapping, taking turns to tread rhythmically on her swollen belly.

With hindsight I might say that this scene was the nearest I got to reality in Africa, the nearest to her people. But what is reality? Is childbirth more real than a cloud of flamingos rising from a lake at dawn, an iron muzzle too burning cold to touch, stars bigger and more brilliant than our own, giraffes galloping in waves through thorn trees, surpassing in grace any human movement—was one experience more significant than another? It could only have been made so by feeling, by an appropriate inner response. All Africa was a dream through which I passed, and have not forgotten.

My uncle, meeting us at the station, looked grave. Little was said till were were seated in the hall. Then, swallowing his drink, he said slowly, as though expecting to be disbelieved, 'I've just heard that an English girl is coming out on the *Llandaff Castle—to marry an Indian*!'

Aunt Grizel sat rigid. She put down her glass untasted. My aunt hated the Indians. When she could speak she said, 'She must be stopped, of course. Fetched off the boat and brought straight here. So that we can tell her what it would mean. She can know nothing. Ignorant, a low type no doubt—but still, a British girl.'

She went to her desk, wrote out a chit and sent for the Head Boy. The chit was to be delivered to Lady Hanbury-Browne—personally, by him. As she got up I saw that her clay-coloured face seemed yellow. With some difficulty she began to go upstairs, turned back and spoke with venom: 'Haven't I always said something disastrous would happen if we didn't keep them down? We got them in to build the railways, now they're buying up the shops. Scum! If we were to leave the country they'd be massacred by the natives within the hour!'

'She's going to have one of her gall-bladder attacks,' my uncle said.

The "natives" were all right; they were like children, specially her servants. And the Arab community understood the British, flattered us, arranged picturesque ceremonies after the Ramadan, very formal, uniforms, medals worn. Rose-water and mint tea in delicate cups which we drank under silk canopies, our feet on priceless carpets. They were rich, but not at our expense. Their leader had been knighted. But the Indians . . . !

After Aunt Grizel had gone up to dose herself with castor oil Uncle Mat told me what he had found out about the bridegroom. His father owned the chemist's shop, and his son had been sent to London University to study law. He had been back some months before sending for the girl.

'I daresay his parents weren't all that keen,' my uncle remarked. 'You realize she'd live in one of those little white houses in Kilindini with God knows how many in-laws, where it's always stifling hot. No white woman would speak to her.' Her life, he said, would be unbearable. Furthermore the white community would be disgraced.

Next morning Aunt Grizel and I were driven to the Hanbury-Brownes' where the important ladies in the British community were gathered together with their tea and cakes. Everyone was temporarily speechless when Aunt Grizel came out with the news, not just because nothing like this had ever happened before, but at the idea that it ever *could*. Then there was a burst of talk, a note of awful, scandalized enjoyment, till my aunt pronounced: 'That's settled then. The ship docks tomorrow.'

She and Lady Hanbury-Browne were to go out in the pilot's launch, bring her back and take her to our house.

'Fortunately the *Dunvegan Castle* comes up from the Cape the following day and she can be put aboard.' The girl's passage home, she intimated, would be paid.

Next day, about noon, I drove down to the port and parked above the quay, blindingly white, where the official car with a flag on the bonnet was waiting. There were the usual groups of people, but I couldn't see if any of them were Indians. I saw the pilot's launch on its way out to where the ship was anchored. Before long the launch returned. My aunt, the P.C.'s wife and a girl got into the car and drove off.

By the time I returned the bride had been put in the bridal suite; whatever my aunt and the P.C.'s wife had said to her, she didn't, understandably, want to come out. She wouldn't eat. At dinner the head house-boy came out with an untouched tray. All that afternoon, lying on my bed upstairs, I had waited, curious, uneasy. By now the enormity of the situation had begun to sink in. Would the bridegroom not come? Surely the Indians would come? But no-one came. Nothing had been said on the subject at lunch.

After dinner my aunt and uncle went out to the Club.

Why did I not try her door, go in openly to see her? The bridal suite was on the ground floor. The grounds were always patrolled by night by an elderly Askari (an old soldier) with a rifle. After he had gone by I slipped out on to the verandah. Through the shutters a light was burning. The heat in the closed room must have been unbearable; I heard the whirr of the fan stirring hot air on the ceiling. Through a gap in the louvres I saw her. She was sitting on the bed under a mosquito net like a veil, clasping her ankles. She had red hair, a great fuzz of it, and she was staring ahead.

Next day she went off. The *Dunvegan Castle* came in soon after dawn, anchoring as usual off the island, as I saw from my bathing place. The pilot launch went out. The ship came into port, but she was already on board, the pilot told me afterwards. Stayed in her first-class cabin, provided by Uncle Mat.

Not much was said, subsequently, and Aunt Grizel's bobbly fringe shook so alarmingly that I never dared to press the question, either with her or Uncle Mat, as to how the Indians had reacted, how they had been approached. The incident had shocked them too deeply, my aunt and uncle, not, I think, only on moral grounds: it was a small crack in their security, the beginning of the end.

But my aunt did tell me later that the girl had worked in an A.B.C. tea shop where students went. It was there that she and her fiancé had met.

Soon after that, just as the rainy season, about which I heard such lowering descriptions, was due to begin, my aunt and I sailed for Durban and the Cape. So that Mombasa remains for me a coral island set in a sea of unvarying blue, where the sun shone punctually from dawn to dusk, and palm beaches stretched to infinity up and down the coast of Africa, specially for the British.

In Cape Town, cashing a cheque in the bank, I saw across the marble floor a most unlikely, dear, tall, comfortable figure—Mr Annan! I rushed across and hugged him. I was nearly home!

Lying sunbathing in an unused funnel on the *Warwick Castle*, blooming, robust as never before, I read a letter from Mother. We were to spend our summer holiday sharing a house with a party of friends in the Salzkammergut. Daddy didn't want to come, but James had just returned from Berlin and she thought he would be the best person to share the driving. I would find

bove: With my sister, Ferelyth, Corringham
oad, Golders Green, 1920

elow: My mother *c.* 1916

ight: My father was good at most games

Above: 'She must be going to be something special'

Right: My parents in the 1930s

Below Left: Liza Lehmann

Below Right: Four generations: my father is in 'Lord Fauntleroy' suit

Above: 'Old Serbia and young Scotland': James with the Patriarch of the Serbian Church, 1917

Above Right: James MacGibbon, Minister of Glasgow Cathedral. 'He came near to scandalizing conservatives in the Church of Scotland'

Right: James's mother, 1910: 'Surprises were what she delighted in'

'I was destined to go to school at St Andrews'

'Chittering bites' at Bamburgh, 1926: 'The three MacGibbon boys' with my mother, my sister and myself. Girl on left a beach companion

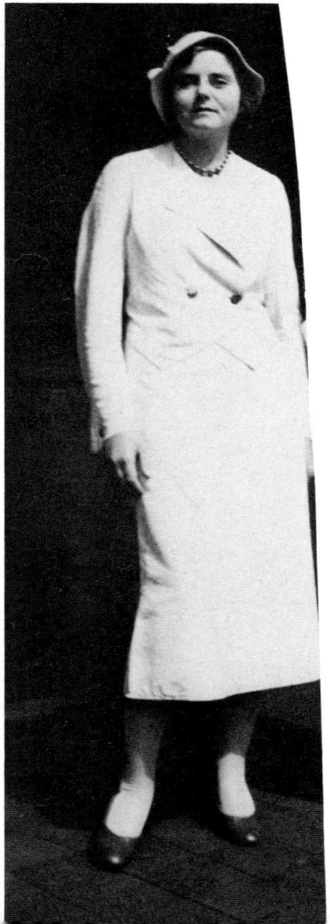

Far Left: My mother and I wedding-bound, I wearing the hat I had on for my tea with John Galsworthy (I could have told him the bird wasn't real)

Left: 'A tussore suit for going up country': Kenya, 1933

Below Left: James with Renata and Helene von Nostitz, Berlin 1933

Below: Helen Pattisson with Hamish, 1937

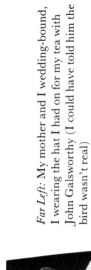

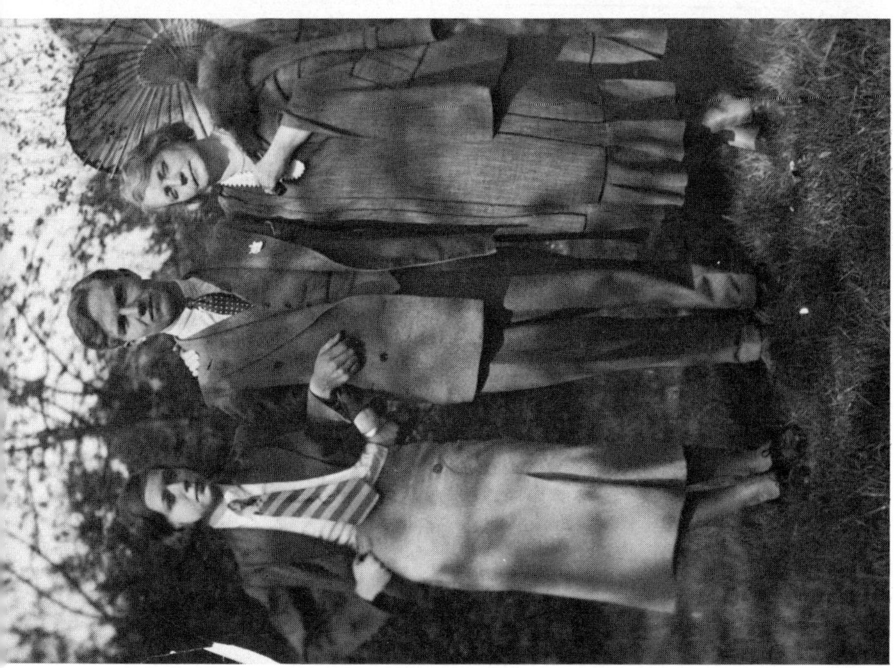

Engagement photographs, 1934

him much changed, she wrote.

And there was a letter from James, posted from Berlin before he left Germany. Belatedly, he had begun to realize what was happening, the seriousness of the political situation, the increasing power of the Nazis.

The morning after the burning of the *Reichstag* he found the Jewish publisher he worked for weeping, his books banned and for burning. James was shaken; but not moved to protest. There were friends in the Nostitz circle, Jews and communists, whose talk was 'disturbing'. Count Harry Kessler, 'an active anti-fascist', got threatening phone calls warning him not to open his mouth against Hitler and 'to stop helping socialists and Jews'. Both the Nostitz sons had been to Kurt Hahn's progressive school, Salem, run on English public school lines. Hahn, on the run, came to the Nostitzes for help. 'I can't forget his hunted, haunted face,' James wrote. Frau von Nostitz, as Hindenburg's niece, seemed to be protected from Nazi persecution; indeed, they courted her.

Even the relatively enlightened Nostitz family wavered. Helene helped her Jewish friends to escape; but still saw 'good things in Hitler', Renata excitedly confessed that she had 'waved a *Hakenkreuz*' at her school demonstration. Her father was shocked; the Nazis, he said, were 'going too far'. Their eldest son, Oswaldt, was a Party Member, a Brownshirt marching in anti-Jewish demonstrations, 'carrying placards outside the biggest store in Berlin'.

James's letter, I noticed, though written in Berlin, had a British postmark; perhaps he had prudently kept it in his pocket.

Without my liberating experience in Africa and James's very different kind of expansion in Germany I doubt if we should have come together again.

IX
Engagement and Marriage

IT WAS NOT so much that James was fundamentally changed, as open to new dimensions of life and art. In the National Gallery he demonstrated how bourgeois the Constables were. Where were the Lochners? The Cranachs? Hieronymus Bosch? We found them disgracefully tucked away. I was enchanted; the weeks before our holiday passed in a warm haze, rapt in the strains of Duke Ellington playing "Stormy weather". Our drive across France took about a week because the car kept going wrong. The first time, in Châlons-sur-Marne, James settled Mother, Ferelyth and me in the best restaurant, presented us with small bouquets and went off to find a garage. Instead of the unspeakable horror such a disaster would have been in my family, there we were having a party. I think Mother quite enjoyed the sense of abandon. He found the best hotel in Rheims and took us there by taxi.

Travelling back to fetch the mended car by train, James and I had one of those rare talks like the ones in Bamburgh, but more intimate. He told me he loved a girl called Winifred who worked in a hat shop—his feelings for Renata were enduring but complicated. I told him about Victor and my resolve never again to expose myself to anything so serious and painful. Which resulted in our feeling easy and comfortable together, and enabled James to hold my hand consolingly without any misunderstanding.

Once on the road again, James wanted to make all speed to Unterach. After leaving Innsbruck we drove through the night, brushing aside Mother's murmurs of dismay. James needed to be sustained with bananas to keep up his strength. As I watched the bananas go down almost without being chewed I thought that nothing but happiness could come from marriage with a man who made such short work of a banana.

However, no sooner had we arrived in Unterach than James announced that he must leave us. He had promised to meet Renata, with friends, on the terrace at Sans-Souci on her birthday. Too astounded to wave, I watched the bus depart. But there behind me stood Count Leo Casa Grande, like everyone else in full Tyrolean gear, only his socks were whiter. In that heady mountain air there was a lot of love around and I can't say I missed James. By the time he returned I was engaged to William, a schoolmaster—at thirty the oldest of the party. He wrote me love poetry in Greek and Latin; and was the origin of my theory that women often fall in love with men on account of their intellect rather than their sexual attraction. James strung along with the two of us, made light of William, and was unimpressed by his ordering an omelette in Latin at a monks' *Bierkeller*.

Nevertheless, after our return to London we entered a period of increasing tension. James's mother was in Spain so he came to us almost every day. It was as though he was rolling all his strength and all his sweetness up into one ball, only not quite like Marvell means. Because he didn't know he was doing it, or who it was for. Nor did I, consciously. Neither of us was in any state to think.

I went for an audition at the Royal Academy of Dramatic Art—the first constructive step taken on my own since leaving school. At RADA I was worked at stretch, enjoying every aspect, physical and mental, of the course. I shared the character parts, Viola in *Twelfth Night*, the old lady in John Van Druten's *London Wall*, with Mary Morris, who went on to a distinguished career.

On Saturdays James called for me on the steps of the Academy after we had both finished work. We lunched at the "Gay Hussar" in Greek Street, where they lit a fire for us in a small room upstairs; afterwards we might go to a movie.

Shortly before Christmas 1933 he borrowed his brother's Wolseley Hornet and drove me up to see Noël Annan, then head of his house at Stowe. We had a lovely time skating and eating scrambled eggs in his study. But James seemed in low spirits. There was some question of William coming down from the Midlands and teaching there, so that we could meet more often. Going home, James hardly spoke. It was then, I think, that I began to sense what he might be feeling for me. Only it was like waiting for some natural catastrophe, a dam bursting.

Two days later I met William in the Belgian Bun Shop in Oxford Street and broke off our engagement. For three days before Christmas James took me out dancing. Every night I wore a different dress. The third night be bought me orchids.

On Christmas night we had a charade party. Everyone except James went home. 'Come out,' he muttered, 'come out on the Heath.'

We sat in the car in the garage. Wordless, he took me in his arms in a grapple-hug and his studs burst out of his stiff shirt. When we were calmer, and had decided to get married, he said we must tell my mother at once.

Waking next morning I felt an extraordinary happiness mixed with a convalescent sense of well-being after a time of strain, not unlike the aftermath of childbirth. A heady sense of right behaviour accompanied my tumultuous feeling for James; I had done more than was expected of me.

We were married on 26 April 1934 at Saint Columba's, the Church of Scotland in London, by George MacLeod, James's father figure. At the Lord Warden Hotel, Dover, there was an enormous fire in the bathroom as well as the bedroom, and the biggest bath towels I had ever seen. The Wolseley Hornet bumped us across France at top speed. In Freiburg our honeymoon was disrupted by a rally of the Hitler Youth, endless cohorts marching by torchlight underneath our hotel bedroom. In the Adolf Hitler Pass we rested so that I could recover my strength on boiled eggs, honey and milk. In Innsbruck, where we occupied the Imperial Suite, all leather padding embossed with golden bees, we threw Marie Stopes out of the window and went to a musical comedy in the little gold and crimson theatre. Called *Die Glückliche Reise*, it was perfectly appropriate: we were sure our life was going to be just that—a happy journey.

But life is not a musical comedy, though for too long we

continued to behave as though it was; and our marriage would have been easier if we had been able to talk more honestly about the problems of life together instead of living each day without reference to what had gone before or what was to follow.

It comes to me as I write: what stupendous lengths people will go to in preserving an ideal as opposed to a realistic view of someone they love! I cannot answer for James; but it was so for me. A relationship rather than an individual is idealized, a received idea of love and marriage distorting whatever true tenderness may lie beneath. And though I had no such serious considerations in mind when I began to write these memories, they turn out to have a discernible theme: a search for some flawed vision, some crookedness traceable from early childhood, which came between us.

Yet all the while, through a labyrinth of confusion and childish madness, a clue of common sense, ultimately of moral sense, the opposite of madness, lay under my hand. I knew what I needed, though I hardly knew what to do with it when I got it.

Though life with the Nostitzes opened James up to a new world of aesthetic response it was no preparation for English middle-class domestic living, any more than my liberating six months in Mombasa. We were both extraordinarily innocent—not just sexually inexperienced, a commonplace then, and perhaps innocence is not the right word: we had no point of reference for our opinions and behaviour except what we got from books and older people. We had few friends of our own age, none that had set up house together. This may have been partly because of our boarding school education, partly because of his mother's fondness for moving house; and because of my family's cut-off life, my father being as near a recluse as my mother's temperament would allow. In short, we took a long time to learn from experience and moved through each succeeding day in a kind of enchantment, elated at the *idea* of being married.

We planned to live in a new, white, cube-shaped house on a hill near Amershan on land belonging to Professor Bernard Ashmole, the archaeologist. His own house, "High and Over", was one of the first to be built by two young architects, Connell and Ward, who have since become famous but were thought at the time dangerously avant-garde: envious, more traditional colleagues, it was said, accused them of putting too much gum arabic in the concrete mix, let alone the foolhardiness of supposing that concrete would survive English winters.

We had all the extras including a goldfish pool dug half in, half out of the house. The idea was that on moonlight nights we would sit on the sofa in the dark and watch moonbeams strike upwards through water into the room. What would happen when a sou'westerly blew was left out of our calculations. We had exchanged contracts and James had given the envelope containing final details to his mother to post before leaving for our honeymoon. On our return we found she had torn it up: 'It was too ridiculous.'

Though James let several weeks elapse before re-establishing relations, she turned out to be right. By the autumn we were set up more suitably in three rooms plus kitchen and bathroom over a grocer's in Little Sussex Place, a charming cul-de-sac near Hyde Park Gardens where Constant Huntington, James's employer, lived. We needed to be within easy reach for it was his policy to introduce the three young men he was training as publishers into the kind of society where, in his view, authors and book-fanciers were to be met with. At least I think that was why, though it may also have been to give them a bit of polish and *savoir-faire*. Having no sons, he may have had a fatherly feeling for them, one of ambition on their behalf as well as his own.

Constant was a Bostonian of extraordinary correctness and propriety. I never saw him express emotion, though a shadow might pass across his clear-cut, soldierly features, a quiver of his small clipped moustache, a narrowing of his pale blue eyes. He held his chin high and his tall figure was so straight he might have worn a corset, and perhaps he did, for he turned, when he had to, stiffly from the waist. He shook hands by passing you from right to left with his hard, dry palm, possibly fearing contamination, though surely also because some small part of his brain was working like photo-electric cells in a factory production line, throwing out the duds.

Such was his preoccupation with his own peculiar brand of distinction that he went so far as to draw James aside at our wedding reception: 'None of these people will be any good to you,' he said. But he singled out James's mother, oblivious of her rather *outré* costume (hearing that my mother was to wear blue she had dashed out to Shaftesbury Avenue for a blue and silver cocktail outfit). She was handsome, she had about her an unconventional distinction; she had also, as he may have sensed, a latent talent, though she did not begin to paint till she was in her eighties. This is to show that he was far from simply being a quintessential snob. His judgement was shrewd and his tastes as a publisher were eclectic, though only someone who knew him much better than James or I did could have fathomed the workings of his mind.

In October 1934, then, we moved into Little Sussex Place, James twenty-two, I twenty-one, and Edith Haskell nineteen. My parents had made only one stipulation: that we should have a maid. Otherwise marriage, it was feared, might prove "too much for me"—a debilitating phrase all too often invoked by my father to damp down my mother's professional life. Having Edith, it may be thought, would have enabled me to continue at the Royal Academy of Dramatic Art where I had made a promising start. But marriage turned out to be a full-time job, run on guidelines suggested by my mother's household.

Edith, red-haired and sturdily built, physically as in character, was young enough to enjoy her position, changing from her green-and-white checked cotton morning dress into a dark green alpaca and coffee-coloured frilly cap and apron to serve our frugal but formal dinner. We used all our wedding presents every day, including our Waterford finger bowls which appeared at every meal including breakfast. We ate off an eighteenth-century satinwood side-table, the only table we had. On Thursdays we sat in the small kitchen, Edith and I, cleaning the silver, while she told me about her work as a stillroom maid for Lady Bessborough near her home in Hampshire. The Bessboroughs ate a lot of spinach which had to be rubbed through a sheet. Edith belonged to the Cyclists' Touring Club and on her days off (one half-day a week and every other

Sunday) she changed into long khaki shorts and Fair Isle pullover. Soon she graduated to the Long Distance Section, and thought nothing of cycling to Bournemouth and back in a day. The next step was a tandem, and romance. She had learnt to cook from her aunt, a first-class cook, and must often have secretly jibbed at my cheeseparing ignorance.

James earned £3 10s a week plus about £300 a year from a trust set up by his mother who also gave him £300 to set up house with. I had the income from a small trust, £37 10s a quarter. The rent of our maisonette was £52 a year, we paid Edith £1 a week and we could have managed quite comfortably had it not been for my inadequate catering. We ate fresh meat at most twice a week, and not much else. A "joint" lasted us from Saturday to Friday.

Occasionally I had someone to lunch and Edith kept her hand in by making gnocchi and crème brûlée. One of my first visitors was Mrs Annan, as I always called her, for she was really my mother's friend. She contrived to slip tactful housekeeping suggestions into our talk, such as the variety to be had from cheap cuts and offal and fresh mince, and how much more tasty and economical they were than the traditional English "joint" leftovers made into insipid mince.

She asked me whether I spent more money on dresses or coats.

'Oh,' I unhesitatingly replied, 'I buy cheap coats.'

'That's interesting. With me it's just the opposite. I buy coats to last.'

Our day—Edith's and mine—was geared to James's return. During our engagement he and I had sometimes met on a weekday, sometimes in unfamiliar adventurous parts of South London while he was learning to be a traveller—now prosaically called a "sales rep"—swinging along with his heavy bag of books, hungry for sticky cakes, in a sober charcoal-grey overcoat with velvet collar and flapping coat-tails, his black Homburg worn at an angle that took the staidness out of it. On Saturdays we met for lunch. And often, lodging near our house, he came to dinner.

But now he came home every evening with a certainty which, as I lay on our rickety Victorian sofa reading French novels or having a desultory go at writing a short story, was as much a happy affirmation of the married state as the possessions which surrounded me.

The significance of possessions in a young girl's marriage cannot be overestimated. Just having so many presents was delightful, beginning with James's heavy fitted dressing-case stamped with unfamiliar gold initials. Though the accumulation of household goods, all, except the satinwood table and chairs given me by my parents, chosen by us both, gave our marriage a solidity, a finality which, but for our youthful confident spirits, might have made us uneasy.

Not that our purchases, mostly second-hand from the Marlborough Galleries, amounted to much, centring round a satinwood baby grand piano, a plain walnut desk, a curly Victorian sofa, and a huge, green boat-shaped French bed painted with tropical flowers and bursting pomegranates. That bed! Seen end-on, bought without examining the mattress which, when unrolled at home, proved to be Heal's best-quality hair. Such was the tenor of our life, a chapter of happy accidents owing nothing to foresight.

On James's return we bathed together in the cubbyhole contrived by the builders under the roof and dined in evening dress, James in a boiled shirt, I in one of the long confections designed and made in accordance with my idea of what a married woman should wear.

Quite often we went out, generally before dinner, in which case I wore a wine-red wool dress and hat to match, with a veil, and soft, black suede gloves, both of which posed fearful problems. Long evening gloves were easy; the hand part was skinned off and tucked up the wrist. But short gauntlet gloves had either to be removed or kept on which, though I understood the latter to be correct, did not come naturally. Shaking hands in gloves seemed rude (a hangover from school where we got an order mark for shaking hands in mittens). As to the veil, it had to be lifted like a fruit cage to get at the mouth. How to deploy glass, canapé, bag and handshaking with elegance? Particularly when introduced to some literary figure—in those early days I was still, in James's words, a "bourgeois intellectual snob" and could come over faint at the mention of a famous literary name. Once, after talking most of the evening to a charming elderly man whose name I had not caught, James told me on the way home that he was Desmond MacCarthy: I had to be taken into a chemist's shop.

I soon ceased to be impressed by literary lions. But Desmond was truly impressive though he might have been surprised to hear anyone say so. He was one of the first people to treat my random observations seriously, taking them up like a craftsman, shaping and connecting, making something of them.

We sat next to one another at a luncheon party given by the Huntingtons for Karen Blixen; Putnam had just published her *Seven Gothic Tales*. There was always an air of improvization when they entertained in their outwardly imposing Hyde Park Gardens house, as though it was not thoroughly lived in (except on the nursery floors where their daughter Alfreda and her nanny lived in ordered comfort. We sometimes went to Sunday tea there and sang hymns with Nanny at the piano). On this occasion there was a hired butler, and Gladys Huntington, at one end of the long table, seemed as usual not quite to know what was going on about her, or rather behind her, for she was too gentle and courteous to neglect her guests. She supplied the warmth that her husband lacked, or could not show, sitting there with a casual grace touched by sadness, a suggestion of hidden intellectual depth, still handsome though her soft brown hair was carelessly arranged, her great smile marred by ill-kept teeth. She was wealthy; and this may have made it easier for her to disregard convention and to loosen herself, sometimes, from their mutual constraint. A friend who knew her better than we did and stayed with her in Italy, which must have been her spiritual home, told us she was bitterly unhappy. She was fortunate in finding fulfilment towards the end of her life in the anonymous publication and success of her long-gestated novel, *Madam Solario*.

At lunch Desmond and I discussed writing. 'Don't,' he said, 'dispise clichés of good pedigree.' We got down to the question of why women write differently from men. He suggested that it might have to do with the difference between our sexual feeling, men's being concentrated, women's more diffused. I remarked that women aren't always attracted by a man's sexual attributes but by his intellect.

This led to an absorbing discussion and I never exchanged a word with my other neighbour, Aldous Huxley. Earlier James and I had stood beside him and his wife on the doorstep staring silently ahead at the door which, as usual at the Huntington's, took some time to be opened. His aloof presence was accentuated by his heavy-lidded eyes and, piqued by being ignored, I recalled Coleridge's Atheist owlet who:

> Sailing on obscene wings athwart the noon,
> Drops his blue-fringed lids and holds them close,
> And hooting at the glorious sun in Heaven,
> Cries out, 'Where is it?'

This extreme reaction may have been prompted by my having heard that the poor man stared at the sun to cure his blindness. Otherwise I can't explain why the words came to mind.

Meanwhile Desmond was conversing with Karen Blixen. *Her* silver-painted eyelids gave her a Basilisk look. At that time metallic paint wasn't commonly used in make-up. I found it fascinating, bizarre, in keeping with the atmosphere of *Seven Gothic Tales*. We came to know her, I got over her strange appearance, and we were friends by the time *Out of Africa* was published. Aunt Grizel in Mombasa would never say what "that Happy Valley crowd" did up-country. One understood that their behaviour was diabolical. Now, reading Karen's version, I knew the truth.

Desmond MacCarthy asked us to tea in his flat in Garrick's Villa near Hampton Court. I embarked, with my customary intensity, on Virginia Woolf's writing. She had her limits, Desmond remarked; she couldn't do businessmen.

'Not businessmen?' I cried fiercely, 'What about Louis? "The great beast stamps" . . .' This was all I could immediately recall about Louis in *The Waves*, but there must be more.

'I love you for adoring Virginia,' he replied, retreating behind his desk, 'have some chocolate cake.'

During lunch on another day Desmond sat next to his wife Molly who was very deaf. She had written two novels some years previously and when one of the guests asked why she didn't write another Desmond roared happily, 'Yes, Molly, why don't you? I have always longed to be Mister Henry Wood!'

'A Bohemian,' he said on another occasion, 'is someone who spreads butter on his toast with a perfectly clean razor.'

Such aphorisms, if that is the right word, came easily into his talk; it may be imagined how attentively we listened whenever we had the chance.

Also in Hyde Park Gardens lived Roland and Jenny de Margerie whom James had known in Berlin. Roland, First Counsellor at the French Embassy, was everything I expected a Frenchman to be. (My short stay *en pension* in Paris had ensured my never meeting one except the tubby *Professeur* at the *Palais de Glace* who taught us the Figure of Eight in between *pots de chocolat* thick as cream, two full jugs per girl consumed at a sitting.) With a mind formed, no doubt, on Cartesian principles, the basis of French education, Roland never had to stop to think, nor wasted a word: information and opinion slid out like billets of polished wood guillotined into equal lengths. He kept up with current publications: books were "useful", "important", "significant", "interesting". Naturally he never read stupid books. At home in France he relaxed in a summerhouse where he played old records and read detective novels. He enjoyed Henry James's *The Turn Of The Screw*. He told James he was bored by diplomacy, or rather by the restrictions imposed by diplomatic life. He was an amiable man; in 1936, when James's translation of Ladislas Farago's book *Abyssinia on The Eve* came out, Roland asked him to lunch at the Ritz. The book was "important" he said.

Jenny was warm-hearted, for all *her* Cartesian intelligence, and her salon was a real salon, not just an "evening", much less a party, but a gathering of people she judged to be "significant", etc, like Roland's books, with the difference that she cared deeply for the people in her collection. If Saint Thomas Aquinas had been available he would have been there along with Father d'Arcy from Farm Street, not because they were fashionable in intellectual circles but because she loved them, revered them, they were of central importance to her.

I now have to ask myself what James and I, with my wine-dark hat and veil, were doing there? The answer must be simply that she liked us.

I so loved listening to French spoken, had so soaked myself in French literature, albeit indiscriminately, that she may have responded to my passion by asking us to meet Paul Valéry. It may be that not many young people in England at the time cared for his poetry. Otherwise she would surely not have taken me up to him and, with the briefest introduction, suggested I should repeat some verses from *Cantique des Colonnes*, which, without preamble, I did. The following night Jenny asked us to dine and go afterwards to see *Romeo and Juliet*. We drank champagne dry as crushed diamonds.

Valéry sat opposite me halfway down the long table, looking even smaller sitting down, eyes bright as a squirrel's. He talked incessantly in a Niçoise accent I could not follow, much to my regret, since his ribald monologue was flatteringly aimed at me.

'Now, Paul,' Jenny would chide him from time to time.

'*Mais je suis mariée*,' I said once, pretending I had not missed a word.

'*Tant pis*!'

Afterwards he sent me a copy of his poems, inscribed '*A la charmante Madame Jean MacGibbon qui dit ces vers, son voisin chez Shakespeare presente tous ses hommages*.' Enclosed was a green postcard on which he had sketched in Indian ink the view from his window at home, a round summerhouse in the garden where he worked.

It was at Jenny's that we met Gérard Boutelleau, London diplomatic correspondent of *Le Figaro*. His father, the novelist Jacques Chardonne, was the author of one of the multi-volume sagas I had taken to Mombasa. But it was an earlier novel, *Claire*, about a young girl in love with an older man, that had caught my imagination. Gérard, too, liked it best. And it was on this basis that our friendship began.

Gérard was not my "idea" of a Frenchman, not strikingly good-looking, tall, and with a long red nose. Nor was his outlook conspicuously "Cartesian". But his ways were not English. An immediate sympathy sprang up between us such as I had never felt before. I cannot say what he felt; and though many years later there was an opportunity to ask him, the moment passed, the question went unasked. There is little doubt that I was in love with him, and that in one part of my mind I knew it; but since I had been happily married for six months such a situation was impossible, did not exist.

This accommodating split-mindedness allowed a friendship to develop which James did nothing to interrupt. He and Gérard got on famously; James could sit puffing his pipe of an evening while I lay on the Victorian sofa with Gérard stroking my stockinged foot as he read Rimbaud and Baudelaire. What we did was to talk, mostly about writing, our own and others'; but with a degree of intimacy and unspoken exploration that I found overwhelming. We once walked across the Park discussing a short story I had written, and back again, and over the Serpentine for the third time, without realizing where we had been. Marriage sets emotions free and allows an expansion of relationships within its framework that an individual may formerly have been unequal to. But it is an indication of our strange, drifting unworldliness that neither James nor I questioned the nature of the bond between Gérard and me.

In one small respect marriage had early on proved disappointing: it was not that James was over-silent; but he was not spontaneously informative. On a mountain path in Austria I said out of the blue: 'Tell me something.' James, startled, asked what?

'Anything.' (I had in mind walks with my father in which we chased Meadow Blues and Meadow Browns—butterflies—compared wild flowers with a pocket reference book, rehearsed battles, celebrated Scottish heroes.)

James was silent.

'What are you thinking?' I asked.

'I wasn't thinking of anything.'

'You mean your mind was a blank?'

'I suppose it was.'

The idea cast a chill over the rocky path. With a mind that was always buzzing, often like a bee swarm gone mad, I could not then conceive how the inside of one's head could be empty.

Gérard shared a flat in Craven Street off the Strand with another journalist, Robert Guillain, who later made his name as foreign correspondent for *Le Monde* in the Far East. Occasionally they breakfasted with us on Sundays, lace mats, finger bowls and all, and we would set off from Waterloo for a walk in the Surrey hills. There was more stimulating continuous talk, dodging among the brambles and yew trees of the Pilgrim's Way, or along Box Hill, ending up at the pub for beer and cheese.

I have remarked that I looked for stereotypes; Gérard, too, was one for stereotypes: himself a fervent anglophile, he had his ideas of typical Englishmen. No doubt, like any newspaper-man, he was assessing, collecting, filing instances of behaviour, idiosyncracies which might come in useful to enliven his reports about "*Queen Mary dans le parc de Kew*"; and "*M. MacDonald dans le cabinet*".

At East Clandon he made a splendid catch. We crammed at the last moment into a crowded carriage, the guard stood ready with his flag, when a small foxy-nosed man opened the door shoving before him the rump of a large dog. In his haste he got his stick caught across the doorway, fell over it, the dog escaped under the train, his master dived after him, whistles blew, shouts, cries, shrieks from a woman passenger, confusion, before man and dog were retrieved. As the train began to move, the woman who had shrieked cried, 'I was sure the dog would be killed!' 'Typically English!' murmured Gérard, delighted with his catch. It may be true that the English, on the whole, prefer dogs to people; certainly dog-lovers put them first.

All that summer Gérard and I continued to meet, and talk; my memory of him is fused with the novels and poetry he put my way, beginning with *Le Grand Meaulnes*. 'Everyone should read it before they are eighteen,' said Gérard. But at twenty-one I was still young enough to enter that enchanted world, move through the cold, spare landscape, the mist-hung forests, all centring on the explosion of surprise, of light, and bizarre fantasy. The last part of the novel loses momentum; I lost interest. I can see what Gérard meant about the book being required reading at the right age, for it is the very substance of an adolescent's inner world and mind, uncertain as between reality and fantasy.

I tried to read more attentively. Had it not been for Gérard I might never have got beyond the first page of Michelet's *La Sorcière* which I found for myself and took down from the bookseller's shelf because of its scarlet leather spine and the bookplate—it was from Arnold Bennett's library. I had a latent interest in and fear of witchcraft, had suffered, as some children do, from the fear that I might be a witch (as some exasperated grown-up exclaimed, 'Jean only has to look at an object for it to break'). Witches, wrote Michelet, had once been beautiful, sybils in Ancient Greece. Their very wisdom made them hated; they were driven into the forest to live on roots and berries. Nor were they malevolent:

> *De sa finesse, sa malice, souvent fantasque et bienfaisante, elle . . . fait le sort, du moins endort, trompe les maux.*

The words themselves were an enchantment, a *soulagement.* I didn't stop at *La Sorcière*, but became interested in Michelet himself and the times he lived through, a more adult way of reading.

On New Year's Eve, 1935, Gérard and Robert gave a party and I broke a previous engagement to go to Craven Street, leaving James to attend a party given by a friend in the War Office. Gérard lit a fire on the tarred roof—how was it that the house didn't burn? I was pregnant, wrapped in a great cloak of midnight-blue velvet, and at the foot of the ladder leading up to the trapdoor Gérard took me in his arms, to my joy, horror, surprise (oh, but could it have been surprise? Had he not nourished me on Baudelaire, Rimbaud, *Le Grand Meaulnes* for just such a conjunction?). And when we were all on the roof with linked hands round the fire he kissed us all, as it seems now a farewell salute. For Hope Leresche was at the party, a tall girl on the staff of the *Morning Post*, whom Gérard subsequently married. Hope's machine-gun French was an eye-opener: she took no trouble to roll her R's, her glottal stops were nowhere. I have since observed that English people who speak the language as fast as the French don't trouble overmuch about their accent, realizing that English throats and teeth are not adapted to the French tongue.

I realized what should have been obvious all along, that I did not come first with Gérard. I came first with James, but having them both, the way we had all three been together, was perfect.

(During World War II Gérard fought with the French Army

in a Cavalry *Groupe de Reconnaissance*. After the French retreat he and Hope met in unoccupied France and they escaped to Tunisia. There he was captured by the Germans and was sent to Oranienburg concentration camp. After the war he worked with Stock, a family publishing firm, and later ran a literary agency with his second wife, and Hope who ran the London end. He wrote five novels and a travel book before his early death from cancer.)

Unlike Gérard we were not politically minded, and learnt nothing from him. Until 1935 James continued to belong to the Anglo-German Club in Carlton House Gardens where we met friends, English and German, whom he had known in Berlin. And in 1934, during our first frolicking summer together, egged on by Alan Delgado who worked with James at Putnam, we appeared as Ascot goers in the Conservative Pageant at the Albert Hall. James wore his thick, hairy, moth-holed Fettesian morning coat and his Fettesian top hat. I wore a long black crêpe evening dress bespattered with tulips and a green chiffon velvet bridge coat.

(James's next appearance on that unlikely scene was in 1948, playing the White Russian General Denikin in a pageant organized by the Communist Party to celebrate the centenary of the publication of the Communist Manifesto.)

But in September 1934 we took part, by chance, in our first political demonstration. Strolling through Hyde Park we noticed a straggling crowd gathering across the grass. 'It's the Fascists!' shouted someone. We pushed our way to the front as the first of the Blackshirt contingent marched past a daïs where Sir Oswald Mosley waited with his lieutenants. Jackbooted, rigid, arms raised in salute, they were a small imitation of the Nazi army we had watched on our honeymoon. Only that display had been dramatically staged by torchlight, the Nazi cohorts endless and in no need of protection. In Hyde Park police marched alongside supported by mounted police who edged us back as the hostile crowd pressed forward. For a second or two we were almost under their hooves; then James picked me up; and the crowd let us through. Afterwards we read that there had been "sporadic violence", eighteen people hurt.

That winter we were invited to a play-reading by an author very different from those we met in Constant Huntington's circle. In 1931 Putnam had published *Hunger and Love* by Lionel Britton, one of the earliest significant working-class writers, with a jewel of a preface by Bertrand Russell. What shocked and chastened me were the details of his life, his empty belly, scraps of food eaten in disgusting cafés or taken home to his filthy lodging house. Keeping clean was one of his passions, getting hold of books another; time and ingenuity were squandered in keeping together his one pair of trousers, his one pair of shoes. *Hunger and Love* was worse than Dostoevsky's *In the Depths* because closer to us, peopling the very streets James passed through on his way to work in Bedford Street. What made me envious was the author's persistence, his power, the extreme physical endurance expressed in the white-hot outpourings of this long, sustained book.

The play-reading took place in a small flat at the top of a building near Wormwood Scrubs. We found the room already crowded mostly with women who seemed to us elderly. He had cleared a small space around him, this spare, strong-looking man with grey springing hair that betokened great energy, his scrubbed open-air neck rising from an open-necked shirt; without preamble, he began to enact his play, *Animal Ideas*. The entire play, about animals fighting and making love, was wordless, carried on in grunts, roars, as many sounds as you might hear at the zoo, and with expressive gestures. Nowadays it would have seemed less strange, and to many people, I suppose, not at all funny. Even, perhaps, material for the theatre. Then it seemed both strange and potentially funny, though naturally, taking our cue from the silence about us, we reserved our merriment till we had left, after joining in the general unqualified praise over cups of strong tea. It wasn't just the play that struck us as risible, but the setting, the rapt attention of the ladies in their knitted jumpers, their glinting spectacles, their respectable middle-age contrasted with the uninhibited expression of the animals' sexual activities.

'There was certainly something in it,' James remarked as we walked in the darkness across a windswept space skirting the prison walls. There was certainly something in the man, anguish, tragedy, a courage that transcended the rigours of his life. Chilled by the alien environment, no longer disposed to laugh at the ladies with whose imagined lives I had briefly identified, I put my hand, as I often did when it was cold, in James's greatcoat pocket.

During that same winter of 1934 Ferelyth, who had just left school, went to Vienna as I had gone to Paris. She had a better time there than I had had in my old-fashioned *pensionnat* with five other English girls and no opportunity to speak French or meet French people. Through Viennese friends James heard about the Döblhoffs who, like many formerly well-to-do Austrians, had paying guests, young people for whom they took reasonable responsibility, seeing to it that they had the friends and opportunities they needed. Our parents thought that Ferelyth should not undertake so long a journey alone and asked me to go with her. The journey was exciting, the huge throbbing Orient Express bearing a list of stations, Bucharest, Sofia, Istanbul, beyond our destination. We travelled first-class. The inlaid wood panelling, the food in the softly-shaded dining car—everything combined to make us feel travellers far from home.

In Vienna the cold was dramatic, only bearable when one was on the move. Immobilized in the *Spanische Hochschule*, where Ferelyth's love of horses took us the first morning, the formal movements of the animals, their hooves noiseless in soft sand, the riders in their Napoleonic hats, all became meaningless, lost in frozen homesickness for James. I doubted if I could stick out the three days arranged for me. After visiting Ferelyth's new 'cello master and seeing her settled in the Döblhoffs' two large, warm comfortable flats with double doors, porcelain stoves and the smell of wax-polished wood, we said goodbye.

That afternoon I went to the Palace of Schönbrunn and stood in the park at sunset, mesmerized by frozen cascades falling from frozen walls. Had James been with me, the winter strangeness of Vienna, the baroque squares silenced under snow, the distant sound of trams, St Stephen's *Domkirche* piercing black against piercing stars—all would have been stimulating and delightful had James been there. I had never stayed in a hotel on my own. The double windows in my room with its baroque wood-burning stove were further insulated by a bearskin, as I found when I opened them. The chambermaid, feeling the draught from the end of the corridor, rushed in and closed them without a word.

Next morning in the Prater Gallery, thinking of James, thinking of our bed with its pink sprigged quilted cover, I began to run as once I had run away from school. I ran through squares, under archways; in an archway I flagged down a young man in a car who drove me to the hotel to collect my bags. Running across acres of railway lines I just caught the Ostend express.

The following morning, which happened to be a Sunday, we got straight into bed and stayed there all day, more for comfort than for sex. The parting had taxed us both severely.

X
London Entertainment and Country Visits

We rarely drank anything but beer, and that only at weekends. But on James's twenty-third birthday I bought a bottle of red wine and asked Edith to warm it in the oven. She brought it in bubbling. And when it was time to leave for the theatre, James's washleather gloves, washed at the last moment and baked in the oven, were hard as boards.

When I wanted to ask friends to tea one of our first differences arose. I had looked forward to Sunday teas at four-thirty, the satinwood table spread with a lace cloth, the gold lustre teapot, the muffin dish and the green and gold tea service from Goode's. But James said this would never do: in Berlin tea parties were never given, at least not before five, and never sitting round a tea table. Sherry must be served, tea and coffee were permissible if I must have them, but served from a dumb-waiter of some kind. We had no side table nor any room for one; so we served tea, sherry and bath buns from the A.B.C., buttered and cut in quarters, off the piano. Great-uncle Alec had given us a nest of tables scaled down on the Russian doll principle; the smallest was inevitably overturned as we threaded our way between the furniture.

Once we gave a sherry party. I wore a scarlet dress with a velvet collar like a monk's cowl and a belt a handspan wide made for me by Ferelyth in gold cloth embroidered with jewels and Chinese dragons. I wish I had that belt still!

We asked everyone we knew, including of course Gérard, Robert, Alan Delgado and another Putnam friend of James's, Teddy Schüller, an Austrian refugee. Teddy, our age, had become an extremely correct Berliner, his long wavy hair brushed carefully back, his manner suggesting restrained enthusiasm. He modelled himself on the head of Ullstein's, the publishers he had worked for in Berlin, and used to practise opening, entering and shutting the door like that august personage.

Another publishing friend who came to our party was John Pattisson who worked for Martin Secker, later to become Secker and Warburg. He brought a contingent of friends, most of whom we had met at his home, among them an entertaining, strange character, Roscoe Beddoes. He could have been a Sydney Smith type of clergyman in the eighteenth century, though on our first acquaintance he had shown no religious leanings. It was at about the time of our party that he surprised us by joining the Roman Catholic Church, entering the Jesuit College in Rome and becoming a priest. His parish was in a remote Welsh village. Looking down from our window after our party we saw John and Roscoe dancing round a lamp-post, Roscoe's coat-tails flying like a rook's plumage in the lamplight.

We saw a good deal of the Pattissons whose way of life was better suited to us than that of the friends we made through the Huntingtons. Helen Pattisson, a close friend of my mother's, was of striking and original appearance with nut-brown skin, dark hair and large expressive brown eyes, who could not but influence everyone who came to know her. Uncommonly tall, she had her clothes designed and made by Liberty's in a modified version of an early nineteenth-century style the Brontës might have adopted, and wore them till they were beyond repair. Striding along in her dark-blue broadcloth coat with its coachman's capes, her sable muff, her buckled hat and shoes, she had the air and character of Charlotte's heroine, Shirley. She sang, though rarely in public, and then to an audience in a small hall; her interest was in Scottish ballads and traditional British and French songs. She was something of a scholar, learning medieval French for her researches into early French music. She had been a serious amateur actress and should probably have attempted a professional career.

Married, gifted middle-class women of Helen's generation seem to me to have been more frequently and worse frustrated than comparable Victorian women. They were on the very edge of change, of advancement and freedom which some of their contemporaries had achieved. Yet middle-class conventions held them back. Helen would not have admitted to having been unhappy; though she did not deny her frustration, she spoke of her relationship with her husband as having been one of exceptional fulfilment. But no-one can thwart talent in themselves without making others suffer.

Her husband died when she was in her early forties, leaving her with very little money. Till then she had thought they were comfortably off. She took her two sons, John, seventeen or eighteen, who left school and started work for Martin Secker, and Alistair, still at Westminster School, to live over a builder's in Holland Street off Church Street, Kensington, where by practising ingenious economies she contrived to live with stylish dash and elegance, holding regular evenings for their friends, including the novelist Angus Wilson who had known John at Westminster. Angus dedicated *The Middle Age of Mrs Eliot* to John and to Helen's memory and I have always thought that Meg Eliot, the chief character in that novel, has something of Helen in her character and circumstances—her husband's violent death, the change from comfortable living to comparative poverty, the sturdy way she coped with these reverses and made the most of her life. (In *The Wild Garden* Angus has, of course, given his own account of the provenance of his characters.)

On 21 December, according to custom, the Pattissons and Helen's sister Madge, a gifted mathematics teacher quite as remarkable as Helen in her own way, all came to dinner to celebrate my mother's birthday. This date, for Ferelyth and me, had always been more significant than Christmas Day itself. From our earliest years she and I had planned and plotted in deepest secrecy: with much ceremony Mother was crowned queen.

On this first birthday in our own home, James, in mutton-chop whiskers, and I in a Victorian crêpe hair fringe, sang a Victorian ballad, "Hail, smiling morn!", and very tricky it was to sing, entailing holding a breath for eight undulating bars. We sang it well; we had practised; no-one ever sang badly for my mother. Alistair played his recorder. And Madge, wearing, as she always did on evenings out, family jewels on her plain dress—Madge, looking not much changed since her Girton days, beamed upon us all.

In addition to London entertainments we sometimes went away for a week-end. (Constant said we mustn't say "week-end" but "Saturday to Sunday". We never remembered.) Bryan Guinness, now Lord Moyne, a Putnam author, asked us down to Biddesden, the grandest house I had ever been in, though he himself was not grand but like a friendly farmer with his out-of-doors complexion. His farm was run by Michael MacCarthy, Desmond's son, and after breakfast, *à la Petit Trianon*, we all went out and made the hay. I have never been at ease in that scale of house and living, though James takes easily to it.

The four-poster bed, the maid in a mob cap and eighteenth-century costume who ran our bath, the servant who laid out James's things—it was not to be missed, none of it. But a day or two was enough. Besides, the place was so cold, specially the stone-flagged hall where we met before dinner. Bryan's fur waistcoat, making him more than ever like an eighteenth-century farmer, seemed, with the women in evening clothes, insensitive. But had it occurred to him that we were cold he would no doubt have provided us all with fur waistcoats. People who live in the country and spend a lot of time outside are notably insensitive to draughts; perhaps we have become so ourselves. One knows where the cold spots are, as visitors do not. It was not till after the war that most country people considered any form of heating in the bedrooms.

We went to stay with Bryan Guinness again in the autumn bringing with us Gaby Schlieper, a tall blonde girl with skin of alabaster purity whom Bryan had met with us at dinner. She was one of James's Berlin friends. Her father was a banker and James remembers men clustering round her not so much for her beauty as because they were disturbed by the rise of Hitler and hoped, through her father, to get inside information.

That visit to Bryan's is memorable for the shoot in the afternoon. I was impressed, slightly dubious, at the familiar way James, who had never shot at anything except a target in the O.T.C.—and he was wonderfully accurate with fairground ping-pong balls balanced on jets of water—joined the others in the gun-room, kitted himself out and chose a gun, squinting down the barrels in a knowledgeable way.

The party was gathered near a hedgerow when James's gun went off. Without a word said, a beater removed a dead rabbit from the hedge. We then formed up, spreading in a long line across the ploughland, and the proper shoot began, with us spectators following in borrowed gumboots, stumbling between furrows and mangold tops. James didn't hit anything else; but when we left, leaving Gaby behind, we took with us a brace of pheasants which had to be accommodated in the cloakroom of the theatre where we went straight from the train to see Dodie Smith's *Call It A Day*. I've told this story not because James cares to ape his betters, to show off or to fool around: he likes to do what he does well. But he also likes to join in with whatever is going on, to be one of the party, which is why he sings hymns loudly but tunelessly whenever we have an occasion to go to church.

The place we went to most often was Windrush, Usula Watson's home at Inkpen below the Berkshire Downs. Ursula was my friend from Hall School days.

Little Sussex Place was not more than ten minutes from Paddington Station. We could ring up the Watsons at five forty-five and by running all the way catch the six o'clock to Reading, change trains and get to Kintbury by seven-thirty. This loveliest of all country stations is hard by the Kennet. On the further bank the Dundas Arms, a fishermen's inn, sleeps in late sunlight. A moment's pause on the wooden platform to take in river smells, shadowed, reedy, trout-harbouring waters. Then down to the level crossing where there awaited Jingle, an ancient Austin Seven covered in faded raspberry fabric, or if there were more travellers a large hardly less venerable open Austin, driven most likely by Ursula herself.

Mrs Watson, her mother, had brought off a remarkable feat of family engineering. When her brother's children were left without parents she and her husband, with four children of their own, had bought a white Georgian house that looked along the Berkshire Downs and there amalgamated the two families, her three girls and a boy, and the Usbornes, four boys and a girl, most at difficult stages of adolescence. There may have been casualties, as in ordinary families; but the scheme worked.

This was the family I should have chosen to belong to. And in some sort felt I did. To be accepted by the self-sufficient Watson-Usborne tribe was a perpetual surprise. Not long ago I asked Dick Usborne if they hadn't thought me rather an oddball. 'No,' he replied, 'we were such oddballs ourselves.'

Mrs Watson was the heart and centre of Windrush; Mr Watson, a genial, scholarly man, presided benignly over her creation. Since his retirement from the Indian Civil Service he had worked for the Save The Children Fund. I never called them "Dorothy" or "Hubert", not just because of convention, rather they symbolized respected parents, part of the security of the place.

From the front door across a gravel sweep an expanse of lawn swept round trees and shrubberies like capes and bays. At the far end were two grass courts where tennis parties were held, with jugs of real lemonade. And over all the long, chalk-backed Downs.

The possibility of war was still far from our minds. How could we have foreseen that some of the players in their white flannels would in five or six years' time be dead? (Yes, some people did foresee catastrophe: but we did not.)

Having unobtrusively settled affairs within doors Mrs Watson spent most of her time in the garden among the fruit and vegetables, producing trugfuls of new potatoes, baskets of strawberries, mounds of raspberries to be eaten with thick cream. There might be twenty or more of us to feed.

When we came upon her she would stop to listen, birdlike, her head on one side, interested in whatever we had to tell her, laughing, it seemed, from the pleasure of having us all about her. Her cheeks were veined like a Beauty of Bath apple. At night in the drawing room, tired by her long open-air day, she often fell asleep like the animals at our feet, lamplight on the fair plaits coiled about her head.

The three Watson girls I had known at school. Their brother Michael and their cousin Margaret Usborne were too young, at first, for us to see much of them. The Usbornes, though outwardly conventional, harboured tumultuous feelings that found expression in varying talents. Dick, the third brother, was my favourite. When moved, his fair skin would go pink up to his prematurely thinning fair hair. This happened when he spoke of writers and writing. He, like Gérard, introduced me to new authors, Max Beerbohm, George Moore—I come upon them sometimes when dusting the books, inscribed in a hand formed by writing Greek.

Dick, as R. A. Usborne, is now well known as author and broadcaster and as an outhority on P.G. Wodehouse. His *Clubland Heroes* was the first serious analysis of the novels of Buchan, "Sapper" and Dornford Yates, exposing their brutality, their anti-semitism, showing how they epitomized a class, a post-war generation. One of Dick's specialities was a succession of long-limbed prestigious girls who at week-ends drove him down in long-bonneted prestigious cars. All the Usbornes except Henry read classics, three of them at Balliol. Henry read engineering at Cambridge. They all played cricket. Michael Watson, fulfilling his father's ambition, captained the Harrow eleven. Mr Watson, that otherwise kindly man, felt immoderately about cricket. His ambition, it was said, had been to father enough sons to make up an eleven. When his wife, in the Indian foothills, gave birth to a third daughter, he telegraphed: "Better luck next time."

The middle-class Englishman's passion for cricket is too well known for comment. But the following story throws a curious light on Victorian ethics. My father, talking about homosexuality, said he'd never come across it at Harrow. 'Except for one chap, Vibart his name was. He was expelled. But not till after the Harrow and Eton match, of course—he was a deadly spin bowler.'

Ursula and Margaret also played cricket well. But, being girls, they didn't count. Margaret took a First in classics at Cambridge. And they all wrote, if only occasional verse. The walls of the downstairs lavatory, smelling of cricket bats, linseed oil, Sanitas, drains, mackintoshes, were papered with parodies in many languages to which guests contributed, celebrating the place, the lavatory, including, I am proud to record—for the standard was high—one of mine, a parody of Matthew Arnold's *The Scholar Gypsy*.

I recall, as I write, the long polished table in the dining room reflecting candle flames from silver candelabra; men in boiled shirts, girls in long dresses. The talk turns on former holidays. (Bathers flashed and tossed in the weir, cars came home from Oxford, from Stratford at all hours, purring cool on a sunburnt skin through moonlit Abingdon. That evening journey marks an August when Tommy brought back Gerda, the German girl he was to marry, and the two sat in front in the open car. I had never encountered so much love in the air. When we took Gérard down he remarked afterwards, 'Why is it that when the English are in love they hit one another on the stairs?')

Two subjects never came up in conversation: sex and money. Only recently I learnt to my surprise that the Usbornes were not well-heeled, indeed what might then have been thought of as badly off. Dick told me he gave little heed to where the money came from. They all worked hard when they came down from university. But somehow money was found to get them there and to fund a pleasant though more carefully economical life than seemed obvious. Good things there were in abundance, plain delicious food, books, music and above all travel. But clothes, especially the girls', were serviceable rather than chic. For occasions such as weddings and the Harrow and Eton match an expedition was made to Elliston and Cavell in Oxford. London was avoided anyhow because, with the exception of Jenny, the family sophisticate, the place made the girls ill. One day in the metropolis and the six o'clock from Paddington found them drained, asphyxiated by London's fumes.

It is curious that, of that very "English" family, all but three married husbands and wives from abroad. Mrs Watson may have had something to do with it. She was an enthusiastic traveller herself; and never happier than when seeing her offspring en route for international holiday camps, walks in the Bavarian Alps, bucketing about Greek islands in a cargo-boat.

Mrs Watson was a rebel at heart. She it was who first introduced us to socialism, saw to it that we were put on the right path when she stayed with us in London and took us to a meeting addressed by Sir Stafford Cripps. I don't know that we had ever before met anyone who actually voted Labour. During the General Election of 1924, when we were at the Hall School, Ursula Watson had astonished and rather shocked me by turning up with a red Labour rosette. At that time I doubt if I distinguished "Labour" from "Bolshevism", brought up on the *Daily Mirror* cartoon "Pip, Squeak and Wilfred" in which a "Bolshie" called "Popski" figured, always with a smoking round bomb like a plum pudding. But a more sophisticated girl, Jean Layton as she then was, coming from a prominent Liberal family and familiar with political issues, shared my incredulity.

As a result of hearing Stafford Cripps, James and I took part in our first house-to-house canvass for the Peace Ballot organized by the League of Nations Union 'to demonstrate the British will to peace through collective security'. Though, in our area, we hardly got past the servants who opened the door, the response was widespread throughout the country and produced an 'astonishing vote for disarmament, the abolition of the private manufacture and sale of arms, and the use of sanctions against an aggressor'.

Already Cripps was beginning to organize opposition to the National Government; soon he would campaign for a United Front, including all parties of the Left.

We had begun, at least, to know whose side we were on.

Nor was our generation politically guilty, as it is accused of being, in protesting against the rise of fascism while opposing re-armament. What we feared was the misdirection of military strength by the Baldwin Government with its right-wing bias against socialism and towards Germany and Italy. National sovereignty, war between nations, war as a political instrument—these were dangerous anachronisms. Only through military power vested in the League of Nations could peace be secured.

Utopian though this may seem, it is still true. Though now in 1984, we may be left with little time to come to our senses.

XI
Pregnancy and Broadening Horizons

My discovery in the autumn of 1935 that I was pregnant came as a surprise to me and to my mother, summoned as usual when I was indisposed. Our elderly Catholic doctor's advice on contraception had been limited.

Mothers and daughters have uncomfortably close intuitions as to each other's feelings: and as I lay in our huge, procreatively painted French bed while the doctor stressed the need to avoid constipation I sensed in her a degree of shock, of perturbation. As to my reaction, I was staggered, never having considered the possibility. James was the only one of the three who was overjoyed. Mother took me to a consultant gynaecologist, fortunately as it turned out. And in a short while I began to enjoy a feeling of achievement, of normality and, above all, status.

Meanwhile, horizons were broadening for us both. That same autumn James had been introduced to Michael Higgins who worked on the *Daily Herald* as a lay-out man, a designer as it would now be called. For James, Michael's job as a newspaper man, putting the paper to bed for the last edition in the small hours and never getting home until two or three o'clock in the morning, was dramatic and above all immediate compared with publishing: he was "in the know", close to the source of political and every other kind of news. Michael and Joan Higgins were the first young married couple we got to know, and our growing friendship opened up new possibilities. Michael rose at noon and as often as not they had friends to lunch, with red wine bought in the Theobald's Road at 2/6 a bottle. Every new experience, even the slightest variation from what I was used to, fairly bowled me over. I had never before lunched on the top floor of a Bloomsbury house; I had never tasted quiche Lorraine; the inner glow from the red wine, the tops of the plane trees visible through small, ill-fitting windows, sparrows pecking crumbs on the sooty sill—all was delightful, strange, enviable: this was how life might be.

Michael and Joan were a striking couple, she more than he, small-boned, dark-skinned, raven-haired, her little monkey face set with blazing blue eyes. Her overspill of energy was spent in organizing other people's lives. I was ready to be taken in hand.

With the Higginses we met writers, painters and journalists like Ralph Parker, round, rubicund, with keen eyes behind his gold-rimmed glasses that belied his apparent leisureliness. He was then running a small advertising agency in the Holborn area. No one knew what goods he advertised but a friend said he 'advertised a whole country—Czechoslovakia'. He certainly had connections in Central Europe for he had become *New York Times* correspondent in Prague when the Germans marched in in 1939. As correspondent of an American paper he managed to stay on and this led to his successful years in Russia as *The Times'* war correspondent. It was Ralph Parker, living in Moscow in 1962, who put James on to *One Day in the Life of Ivan Denisovich* by Alexander Solzhenitsyn. James was working for Victor Gollancz, who published it, in Ralph's translation, early in the following year.

And there was Claud Cockburn whose cyclostyled news-sheet *The Week*, typewritten and printed in sepia ink on yellow paper, had expanded from a minute circulation to being required reading for politicians, industrialists, civil servants and in the chancelleries of Europe. Nothing escaped Claud's scent for political scandal, from the latest unpublished gossip about Edward VIII and Mrs Simpson to the inner workings of the Labour Party. James heard Kingsley Martin once charge him with: 'But Claud, that story of yours was only a rumour!' 'My dear Kingsley,' Claud replied, 'without rumour there would be precious little news.' He had been on the staff of *The Times* (at the same time as Graham Greene) and had served his term in their Berlin and New York offices so he was well placed to exchange information with leading political correspondents of European newspapers. What we marvelled at was his incredible energy, allowing him to combine running *The Week* with writing for the *Daily Worker* under the pseudonym of "Frank Pitcairn".

Claud may have had a bloodhound's scent; but he didn't have the anxious wrinkles, the droopy chops of that animal. Erect, tall, swift-moving, his was the elegant panache of a labrador, with his trilby worn at an angle that commanded attention if not admiration. Resilient, reckless but shrewd, with an address when dealing with superiors which just fell short of arrogance—is it fanciful of me, brought up on my father's admiration for Scott and Stevenson, to see there something characteristic of the Scots, of those who have made their way in the world, and throughout the world? I am thinking now of James whose carefree behaviour, while endearing him to his fellow employees, has sometimes been misinterpreted by his employers as careless effrontery and contempt, masking ruthless ambition. Whereas the very opposite is true: he has too little wish to dominate, and will go to excessive lengths to be liked, to be approved of.

Joan, who shared some of Claud's characteristics, was also of Scottish extraction. Her father had been a soldier serving in India and this showed in her bearing. For one thing, if we must have military services, she liked to see them well turned-out. James's sailor brother George, stationed at Chatham, invited us to dinner in the Mess on a special occasion and, as I was laid low with some indisposition, she went instead, driving James down in their open Lancia Lamda, a fast, boat-shaped car of a new design. In spite of speeding they arrived late, which James can't stand, but which left her unruffled. She had chosen, as suitable to the grandeur of the event, to wear the dress she had once worn when presented at Court with the Prince of Wales feathers in her hair. As James and George escorted her up the imposing staircase, her satin train draped over her arm, she remarked without lowering her voice, 'Isn't it splendid that all this belongs to *us*!'

One memorable evening Tom Harrisson, a young anthropologist, turned up at the Higginses, bursting into their small sitting room flanked by several young men like a bodyguard, slightly rumbustious in their confidence. I thought him, at the first meeting, overbearing, unlikeable, but he was certainly charismatic. Michael believed that his new organization, soon to be called Mass Observation, was going to produce a revolutionary change in our thinking and might even bring about a change in society. Tom, with the poet Charles Madge, planned to use anthropological techniques to study our own people, living among the group to be studied, identifying with them, recording their reactions but not trying to quantify or codify human behaviour. They wanted to find out "what made people tick". At first they worked in their own ways: Charles Madge, pale, dark, quite my idea of a poet, had advertised in the *New Statesman* and other newspapers for people to write in about what they were thinking, feeling, doing, saying about trivial matters as well as great events like the abdication of Edward VIII. He got an astonishing response from all quarters. A panel of observers was formed who wrote in regularly.

Meanwhile Tom took a job in a Lancashire cotton mill near Bolton. Later he rented a small house in Bolton and there summoned friends, like the Higginses, to work for him. A full-time staff of anthropologists was to be set up in three areas, Liverpool, London and Bolton—or "Worktown", the name Tom used in the book he wrote for Victor Gollancz's Left Book Club. But anyone could volunteer to be an observer; no special training was needed. The work could be done in their own time—the flexibility of the scheme was part of its ingenuity. (During the war Churchill consulted Tom Harrisson to sound out public morale.)

I tend to look back on the late thirties as a grim time, a time of mounting stress, as indeed it was. But the whole decade was a period of original thought and invention in science and the arts, revolutionary ideas, new concepts, the breaking down of barriers in the mind and between cultures. The young men who started Mass Observation, "the Science of Ourselves", hoped to dispel the received ideas on which the majority were fed by press and radio through the free exchange of knowledge and understanding between classes. Europe, perhaps the world, was heading for disaster; only ignorance and apathy, they believed, prevented us from mobilizing informed opinion.

And if this sounds condescending, over-serious, what struck me at the time, listening to their talk, was how liberating their experience was, what fun they had on their serious assignments!

James and I didn't volunteer for Mass Observation; but no doubt the ferment of new ideas simmering in the Higginses Bloomsbury eyrie contributed to his dissatisfaction with his working life. Like most people of buoyant temperament, James is subject to fits of depression, most often in the early spring. One bleak evening he came home almost prostrated: he flexed his fingers and spread out his hands; the fingers were bloodless, the nails blue. He could not, he thought, continue in publishing.

There were practical reasons to justify this uncertainty. His salary at Putnam, though risen to between £5 and £6 a week, would hardly cover our expenses when the baby arrived. And there were frustrations at work which he had not yet learnt to tolerate. Perturbed by his dejection I asked what he would like to do instead?

Influenced by Michael Higgins' life in Fleet Street, 'a tremendously exciting place where there is urgent action in contrast to slow-moving publishing', he replied that he thought he would like to go in for journalism.

It thus happened that soon afterwards we went to consult Sir Michael Sadler, now married to Miss Gilpin of my Hall School days.

After his retirement as Master of University College, Oxford, they had bought a house in Old Headington big enough to take his collection of paintings. Most of them were Post-Impressionists, many familiar from my school days in the early twenties, when Miss Gilpin had either borrowed the originals or showed us reproductions. But Matthew Smith was new to us and we came away inspired by the colours used in his large paintings of nudes, his deep sea-green blues and flaming reds. In a Bond Street gallery we found a small painting of his, a French landscape of a muddy road winding away between an avenue of fruit blossom. We went back and back to look at it, wondering if we could scrape up the money. We could have had it for thirty pounds! But that was over half a year's rent.

Sir Michael gave James an introduction to the editor of the *Times Of India*. And for a time we thought seriously about the idea; I was ready to sail for India, and with my tropical experience didn't feel there would be much difficulty in kitting ourselves out.

But common sense prevailed; and Erskine Hannay, my early love in the Navy, now a director of Morton Sundour, the textile firm, got James the job of advertising manager. James came home every day full of enthusiasm. Alistair Morton, Erskine's brother-in-law, who had just been made Managing Director, was, James said, 'in his way a visionary, on the side of the angels—the Modern Movement'. He commissioned furnishing fabrics designed by the leading artists of the time. James, who knew little about advertising, less about furnishing fabrics, soon found his way about, drawing up advertisements, laying on exhibitions in the showrooms of Edinburgh Weavers, a subsidiary of Morton Sundour specializing in fine quality fabrics, and in Gordon Russell's furniture shops. He engaged Mischa Black, the architectural designer, to design the Morton Sundour stand at the British Industries Fair and organized the general display in the furnishing section. For the first time, textiles were shown as used in rooms instead of as rolls of cloth hung loosely side by side. Haynes Marshall, head of Fortnum and Mason's furnishing department, was in charge, and James remembers him asking for 'a much limper satin—like a French letter after use'.

One of the last parties we gave before leaving Little Sussex Place was on the occasion of George V's funeral in January 1936. From our roof a close view was to be had of the procession on its way to Paddington Station.

We marshalled our small gathering, put up the fire escape and opened the trap door. Instantly everyone was smothered in clouds of floating seeds—I had stored some bulrushes from the Kennet up there and forgotten them. Brushing ourselves down we crawled through the hatch and disposed ourselves on the leads in time to hear Chopin's Funeral March in the distance.

By the time the cortège appeared they rounded our corner at a relatively brisk pace. The procession seemed endless and perhaps the quickened pace had to do with keeping it moving, as soldiers or marchers on a demonstration close their ranks.

Had we known this was to be the last time the kings of Europe were to be assembled in their Ruritanian uniforms the scene would have had an added poignancy, a terror of the wrath to come. The military band should have sounded the trumpets of Verdi's *Dies Irae.*

I have always loved ceremony, pageantry rooted in tradition, however much this is at variance with my political beliefs. In spite of the unanswerable reasons against keeping on with kings and queens I would rather have a monarchy than a presidency if only because of the drabness of presidents and their wives at public functions. The perpetuation of symbols such as the Cap of Maintenance, part of the ceremony at the re-opening of Parliament, so old that no-one knows its meaning, may help to shore up a social system we abhor; but it is also possible that as unconscious symbols their deeper, unknown meaning may be stabilizing in effect, as they are to me. I make no attempt to reconcile two irreconcilable beliefs. When Elizabeth II was crowned I watched the entire ceremony on a borrowed TV set, and wept when the Westminster boys cried '*Vivat!*'

While James's life was broadening out, mine was, so to speak, deepening as my pregnancy drew to its end. Because of my quirky wish to return to Hampstead Heath before the birth, we decamped to a furnished flat draughtily exposed to east winds across the Hampstead Heath Extension. Here Mother and Edith and I furnished the nursery with a borrowed cot draped in layers of primrose muslin, a folding bath, a Moses basket for daytime use and a covered basket containing everything a baby could need down to a tin of baby powder. The chest of drawers was soon filled with baby clothes called a layette, all provided by Mother; this June baby was to wear a Chilprufe vest, two sorts of nappy, flannel petticoat, lawn petticoat and long dresses of the finest drawn-thread voile with satin ribbon threaded through the waist. Endless matinée coats and bootees were soon contributed. The Vyella nightdresses, to everyone's surprise, I decided to make myself.

Again, material possessions were a delight and a reassurance—a reassurance that the baby would presently be born. I had none of the fears that some pregnant women have, fears about labour, about the child's normality. But though he was kicking and alive inside me it seemed impossible to imagine him outside, lying in the cot.

We bought the pram in Harrods, coach-built, a handsome object, light as a phaeton yet durable, as time was to prove. Did we want a monogram on the side? I would ask my husband, I told the assistant, and rang James at work. 'Of course not!' he replied. But later rang back and said we could have our initials, but in Eric Gill type. Harrods had "J.MacG" put on it in ivory Gill Sans.

I had the gall to ring up the Truby King Mothercraft Training Centre in Highgate: 'I believe you run a six-week course in looking after babies. Can I send my maid along?'

'Why don't you come yourself?' was the restrained reply.

So I did. My introduction to Cromwell House is a further example of how we both—James and I—sometimes arrive at sensible decisions obliquely and for the wrong reasons.

I had none of the feelings some girls have for babies; I had never liked them and had avoided looking at my newly-born sister. As a small child I associated babies with baby birds which I was afraid of—someone had made me touch one, featherless, bluish, squirmy, horribly vulnerable.

But the pragmatical atmosphere of Cromwell House, run by a remarkable woman, Miss Mabel Liddiard, soon dissolved any such lingering fantasies and by the end of the course I felt reasonably confident in handling the newly born, bathing, feeding and changing them. Above all I was determined to feed my baby—at that time, for middle-class mothers a novel, to many a disgusting idea. (My mother never got used to watching me breast-feeding.)

By 1936, through Mabel Liddiard's book, *The Mothercraft Manual*, Dr Truby King, a New Zealander, had become the Dr Spock of his day for a generation of middle-class British mothers. (He had worked in the East End of London and his method was designed with working-class mothers in mind.) Everything we needed to know, much of it revolutionary even in the thirties, was set out clearly and simply, our daily routine laid down to the last detail. The Doctor must have been something of an obsessional; his standards of hygiene were surely impracticable in the long run whatever one's class. Jocelyn Herbert, whom we came to know when we moved to Barnes, herself about to be married to Anthony Lousada and contemplating motherhood, took fright at the paraphernalia on the trolley at my elbow, the bowls, swabs, distilled water for wiping nipples, jars of this and that, a kidney bowl . . .

But I may have interpreted the Doctor too rigidly in the light of my own predilections, or was just in a muddle as when reading the instructions on ventilation: instead of placing the screen between cot and window I put the cot between window and screen, directly exposed to damp and fog. Our first-born grew up remarkably resilient.

At Cromwell House we were taught a foolproof way of folding and tucking a baby into a neat cellular-blanket parcel, loosely warm inside, firm without. After his ten o'clock feed the baby was put where he couldn't be heard, and the mother had an undisturbed sleep till the alarm clock went at six, secure in knowing no physical harm could come to him. Babies were fed by the clock, every four hours—and no night feed.

Harshly though this reads, the mother at least had enough sleep, enough milk and was ready for another day, her anxieties lulled by the regularity of the routine. By modern standards our baby was underfed; the patent New Zealand Cream intended to supplement the mother's milk was hateful stuff both to the child and to the mother who tried to administer spoonfuls. Mixed feeding, introduced at about six months, was laborious; there were no convenience foods and every scrap of spinach and carrot had to be rubbed through a sieve. By that time, too, the baby had learnt enough to reject new tastes.

More damaging were the Doctor's notions about sex. Babies, he stressed, must not be kissed too warmly or too often. Apart from the danger of infection, undesirable sexual feelings would be aroused in the infant. Other mothers of my generation seem to have interpreted the idea according to their temperaments. I can't believe I kept up this distancing for long. James never did, calling the idea 'great nonsense'. Nevertheless, as much because of my own nature as Truby King's, I deprived us both, our son and myself, of pleasure. I brought him up as I play Bridge—by the book. But without the book I could never have managed at all. Mother, when told I intended to look after my own baby, dropped her customary restraint and expressed incredulous alarm. However, Edith was there, and James, and later, when I became ill or collapsed, Mother had a substitute ready.

James didn't allow his new job to interfere with his happiness at the prospect of becoming a father. The alternation between work and increased domesticity suited him. While I embroidered cream Vyella nightdresses he read Trollope's *Doctor Thorne*, or Cecil Day Lewis's *From Feathers to Iron*, a series of poems which paralleled our own experience of first love and the coming of a child. From him we went on to Auden, Spender and other thirties' poets who reinforced our embryonic political consciousness.

Those last weeks were passed in a summery haze; I slept a good deal, dropping off anywhere, in a grassy hollow in the Heath or by the River Kennet. Fishing, James decided, was the very thing for a pregnant father. On the advice of Joan Higgins, herself an angler, tackle was bought at Cogswell and Harrison and whenever we could we spent Sundays by some stretch of water.

A single, unaccountable ripple disturbs the memory of that tranquil waiting time. As we walked alongside the towpath between the Kennet and the canal one afternoon in May, I was struck by the converging lines of the canal flanked by straight hedges and flat water meadows open to the skies in the late afternoon. James is like the canal, I thought. And those converging lines oppressed me with a sense of my own devious nature. 'I must learn to grow more like him,' I wrote in my notebook, 'or I shall lose him. And I shall deserve to lose him.'

But James is not like a canal; he has his own complicated deviousness. And such trouble as we have had has resulted from not seeing each other clearly, as separate individuals, but as objects of each other's idealization. There is cruelty in clinging to a false view of anyone; expectations are aroused which cannot possibly be fulfilled; and a state of tension is set up which can only weaken a relationship.

Except for the fortunate few who attended the clinics founded by Margaret Morris, routine antenatal care did not exist. No preparation, no exercises, no regular blood tests or urine tests. Childbirth had not grown safer or easier since my mother's time when her confinements had so terrified her that our pregnancies—my sister's and mine—filled her with dread.

Not knowing what to expect I let my body swell with fluid till my fingers were like sausages, my eyes half closed. The first intimation that I might be ill came when I went over to Kensington to lunch with Helen Pattisson. Struck by my breathlessness she made me lie down, noting signs of illness with a fresh eye. Our GP came and put me to bed till it was time to go to the nursing home to have the baby induced. The induction failed; and Mr Grey, no doubt summoned by my prescient mother, performed an emergency Caesarian. Hamish was born on 25 June, 1936.

Next morning I sat up and fed our son. He weighed five-and-a-half pounds and his mouth was almost too small to fit over the nipple. Being a Caesarian baby his head and features were perfect. A normal birth can be a shared experience creating the first bond between child and mother; but for me it was feeding him that released maternal feelings.

There followed a time of unclouded happiness and fulfilment. My room was on the ground floor and in the evenings James crossed the grass and entered through the window, staying till dusk. Hamish, not treated in those days as being "at risk", was put under the open window in his cot, and before long the elegant pram was wheeled on to the lawn with all its trappings including a tussore silk scallop-edged canopy lined with green.

When the time came to leave I convalesced for three weeks at my parents' home. They had moved from Frognal to a house in Heath Drive which, without the romantic corners and odd staircases of The Oaks, seemed at last to be the kind of house which my father could tolerate and which made my mother happy. It was spacious, foursquare and with a whole floor for the maids on whom my mother doted. Here Nurse Bunn, a monthly nurse, was installed. And Helen Pattisson came to stay and shared the spare room with me. James came over the Heath, morning and evening. Hamish and I were in clover. Ferelyth, now at the Central School of Art studying drawing and sculpture under John Skeaping, lived her own life in two rooms at the top of the house. My father looked into the spare room from time to time, affectionately amused. But it was between us four women that a continuous baby worship was carried on. The celebration began at six a.m. when tea was brought in,

Helen sat up with her thick black plait, my mother in her dressing gown sat on the end of her bed and Nurse Bunn appeared with Hamish. Ivy B. Bunn came from Norfolk and she was like three buns of diminishing size, one on top of another. Her red cheeks shone, her blue eyes were as bright as her blue uniform; she wore a snowy apron and a Quaker-plain cap.

At the end of our blissful prelude, Hamish and I returned to Heathcroft and he was introduced to life outside the walls of Eden. I pushed the pram over the Heath, continually uncovering him and feeling his feet, appealing to passing Nannies to say if they were the right temperature, while Edith did the hard work and brought him to me from his lonely room every morning at six.

By now James was earning nearly £1,000 a year, wealth compared with the £5-£6 a week he had earned at Putnam. The time had come to set up in a more permanent home. Our choice was not a happy one. I have never, until late on in life, known what I wanted and often made a punishing decision—self-punishing, thus involving those nearest to me. Riverview Gardens was not a place I could ever have been happy in.

Before moving from Hampstead we hired a car and took Hamish to Windrush for the week-end, plus cot, bath and folding pram. He was the first Windrush baby of the new generation and received with fitting acclaim. Mr Watson wrote verses of welcome in English and Latin; the Esse stove was lit in the best spare room; and his bath ceremony was attended by the entire household and privileged friends. Michael Watson and his friend Nico Henderson (now Sir Nicholas Henderson) formed a Heavy Rescue Squad, wearing protective clothing and armed with a stirrup pump. It was about the last carefree, larky, non-political outing before we were engulfed by the seriousness and stress of the coming pre-war years.

It tickles me to think that Hamish was once so rudely bathed by—at the time of writing—our Ambassador in Washington.

XII
The Spanish Civil War

We wanted to live in a flat without stairs. But this conflicted with my hankering after a top floor, thus cancelling out the first reason, for the flats had no lifts. Also living in South London was thought to be cheaper. But people who live in North London think that South London is at the ends of the earth and unhealthy at that, low-lying. Hampstead carries this belief to excess. When we first married we had thought of taking a house in Paulton's Square, Chelsea. But my mother exclaimed, 'Oh, no—it's so near the Brompton Chest Hospital!'

Riverview Gardens is a redbrick, three-storey block of flats with communal gardens running alongside the towing path up to Hammersmith Bridge. Our sitting room looked north across the Thames with a view of Manbré and Garton who processed sugar and animal feeding stuffs. Also a depôt where London's refuse was tipped into barges. Keen winds blew almost continuously from the north and east and the combinations of smells and dust may be imagined. I was homesick, cut off from my family, disorientated. But we were also cut off from our Sussex Place life and its outdated associations. With the birth of our baby our own life was in some ways enlarged. Riverview Gardens was where our political life began. With parenthood comes a sense of the future.

We had come to realize the full threat of Hitler's rise to power, as our families did not. My father reflected the views of most businessmen in regarding Communist Russia as the real enemy and in looking forward to the *Drang nach Osten*. Nazi Germany was seen as a bulwark against Communism. Hitler and Mussolini had much to recommend them; they had brought order out of chaos. Hitler's extra-territorial ambitions, his cries of *Lebensraum!* were ignored.

We had grown up believing there would never be another world war. The Sino-Japanese war, the epic Long March, stirring in their heroism, were geographically far away. The Italian invasion of Abyssinia carried the threat nearer home. What shocked us out of our inaction was the outbreak in 1936 of the Spanish Civil War, brought to our doorstep by the formation of the International Brigade and the departure of volunteers, some younger than ourselves.

All mothers faced with the threat of danger feel a biological need to protect combined with a painful vulnerability. But for me the external threat coincided with an internal crisis. While I am pregnant I feel well, filled, fulfilled: but after the birth empty, scraped out, raw. To this unconscious state was added the fact of Hamish being a first baby, the loss of my freedom, the burdensome realization of his dependence on me: shut up together in his new nursery with its modern, astringent version of a nursery wallpaper, the cold expanse of blue lino, the Morton Sundour washable rug in front of the nursery fireguard, I felt older at twenty-three than I feel now, forced to be adult by motherhood. Before his birth I had had dreams of forgetting to feed him, of losing him. These were groundless fears: my breasts filled with milk every four hours as punctually as Truby King would have wished. As to losing him it seemed to me that we should be inseparable for countless years to come; in this sense of timelessness I was as much a child as I had been my first day at school. And there were more subtle emotional confusions, feelings of pride, of amazement at having produced anything so perfect, fear of harming him, and deeply buried in some split-off part of myself a spoiling envy of my own creativity.

Though small and by today's standards underfed, Hamish was adequately well-covered at eight months with the clear skin of a breast-fed baby and shining dark-brown eyes. An easy baby too, lively and responsive. And he hardly ever cried even when he was put out for hours alone in his pram, three floors down, in the communal gardens with privet hedges that flanked the river. How could I not love him? No doubt I did, but in such an offhand way, inattentive to all but his physical needs, unobservant, letting pass the signs of development that need response at the right time and which are among the rewards of parenthood, mitigating the inevitable boredom.

James loved him with all his heart, prepared to tend him as no other fathers we knew at the time would have dreamt of doing; they did not even push prams for walks on their own. James changed and bathed him and helped to mix-feed him when, belatedly by today's custom, we began inserting spoonsful of sieved spinach and carrrot and egg yolk into his unwilling mouth. So, between the three of us—for Edith played her part—he had not too bad an early start, though I think James, who had never been played with much in his own childhood, relied on loving him, and tossing him and catching him: it must have been like being cared for by an elder brother and sister.

Edith, I think, would have liked to have more to do with Hamish. But she had her work and I had mine was how I looked at it. Besides, Edith was old-fashioned in her views: 'Master him,' she would say, 'or he will master you.' The strange fact is that I was jealous of anyone so much as touching him, determined to "bring him up" on my own. When Mother came she held him beautifully, but not very closely; she could not quite accustom herself to his being a boy with a boy's anatomy and had mixed feelings while watching him being bathed, worse sensations when I let him run about naked in summer. As to "mastering" him I masterminded us both, living by the clock from six in the morning when the alarm woke me till ten-thirty when he was banished to his single room.

And it was upon this nursery scene that the Spanish War broke, wave upon wave with increasing ferocity, till we could think of almost nothing else. It was the Siege of Madrid that fired our imagination. War correspondents like "Frank Pitcairn", Bill Rust, William Forrest, fighters as well as journalists, sent back reports of hand-to-hand fighting in the streets and parks and suburbs, of the University holding out as a citadel, of bloody cobblestones and running gutters, of extremes of heat, cold, hunger, fatigue, of civilian life somehow going on, of air-raids, people sheltering in the Metro, photographs of children's corpses.

Such scenes have become commonplace in the world in which we now live; but at the time the shock was fresh on our minds. We wanted somehow, in however small a way, to become involved.

The local Labour Party secretary in Barnes put us off by his cool reception, counselling moderation: 'We must learn to walk before we can run.' A caution which reflected the official Labour adherence to the policy of non-intervention.

So we turned to the Communist Party.

Our first contact with the Party had been on Hampstead Heath when we strolled over to an open-air meeting about the Spanish War near the White Stone Pond and stayed to listen, held by the speaker's clear exposition and rousing call for support.

A more immediate influence was our membership of the Left Book Club, that mushrooming enterprise in which Victor Gollancz used his genius as a publisher and entrepreneur to further his political beliefs. The volumes, "Book Club Choice" and "Alternative Choice", arrived with persecuting regularity, demanding to be read.

In the spring of 1937 we went with the Higginses to the first Left Book Club rally in the Albert Hall. The place was packed out to the huge domed roof, tier upon tier, as I remembered it from the time when as a child I had been taken to hear Coleridge-Taylor's "Hiawatha" and the Easter ritual of Handel's "Messiah". There was a Messianic fervour in the high-pitched expectant murmur, the hush as the speakers came on to the platform, the acclaim as each one finished speaking.

The occasion of the rally was the launching of the Popular Front movement in Britain, a movement to link all parties of the Left in the fight against fascism that had begun in Spain and taken shape in France under Léon Blum, Prime Minister of the Popular Front Government.

It was here, in the Albert Hall, that I first felt the heady inspiration of belonging to a great concourse of people all going one way, all with the same aims—the overthrow of Baldwin's National Government, the reversal of the infamous non-intervention pact which denied military aid to the Loyalists, and the defeat of the Spanish Nationalists and their fascist allies before the whole of Europe was engulfed in war.

Long ago, in my grandfather's house, I had learned that

"there is a right and wrong in politics and that difference is absolute".

At the end an enormous collection was taken, conducted from the platform by Isobel Brown with a technique that was to become famous.

'Cheques first—who'll send one up for £100? Ah, here it comes!'

Fivers, pounds, ten shilling notes, silver, IOUs flowed in, material evidence of the strength of the Popular Front movement.

The next box to ours was occupied by a soldierly-looking man and his wife whom Joan Higgins had introduced as "Dulcibella and Oliver". They had a private plane, she said, and when swift transport was needed, when, for example, an edition of the *Daily Worker*, printed on the presses of the *Manchester Evening News*, had to be got to London—and Tom Wintringham and his motor bike and sidecar no longer on the road, for he was fighting in Spain—then, she said, Dulcibella and Oliver were instantly on hand. I never heard them spoken of except as a duo. The climax of the meeting came when we rose to sing "The Internationale", arms and clenched fists outstretched in the communist salute. I felt a fleeting embarrassment, perhaps because of hallowed early associations with the Albert Hall, Handel and "Hiawatha", but this was dispelled by a leftwards glance and the sight of that manifestly upper-class pair standing as rigidly as though singing "The King". And I let myself go on the tide of communal emotion, the first of what was to become a habitual experience.

Thus it was that I absorbed John Strachey's *The Theory and Practice of Socialism* while feeding my baby, of all the perverse things to engage in while supposedly consolidating our relationship. I did not enjoy it in the least, nor, surely, did Hamish. "Blessed be the Babe", as Wordsworth so percipiently observed, "who with his soul Drinks in the feelings of his Mother's eye!" There was none of that in Riverview Gardens.

But I did, by painful concentration, grasp certain lasting truths, practical elements such as the Theory of Value, the general truth that raw materials are only of value when worked on, that workers without capital have only two assets—their hands and brains. Most easily of all, the light broke upon me that money as a means of exchange is useful, but as a commodity is at the root of our troubles.

In February 1937 we wrote to King Street. The secretary of the Barnes Communist Party called to see us, and we joined the Barnes Branch. Frank Paterson, "Pat" as he was known, worked for the *Daily Worker*. He came from James's home town, Glasgow.

Margaret, Pat's wife, had a son eight months old, the same age as Hamish. We went to tea with her, and it was probably the first time I have ever been socially in a working-class home. Their two rooms were bare except for essentials, a table, four chairs, a bookshelf of Penguin paperbacks and Marxist Classics, one easy chair—these are the details I remember. The Patersons were poor even by the standards of the time. The *Daily Worker* didn't pay much and sometimes, if they were going through a bad patch, nothing. So much for "Moscow gold", at least for the employees. In addition to his lean look of early poverty and a mouthful of cheap false teeth (soft water and poor diet rotted Glaswegians' teeth), this young father was marked by an honourable spell in prison, taking the rap for some infringement of the law by the *Worker*. The staff took it in turns. Margaret had fair hair, finely modelled bones, fair skin you could have shone a candle through. No sign when we first met of the flush said to be a symptom of the tuberculosis that killed her some ten years later.

Three of her own family died of TB. They were a remarkable lot, the Elmses, and getting to know them did more for my political enlightenment than any amount of theory. Three of the four would have qualified for a university education today. Fred, the eldest and strongest, used to say that he would like to have gone to university if it had not meant his being cut off from his class as, then, it would. He was a skilled engineer. And his stylish Irish wife, Maisie, had an easier life than the others. She even went to a Health Farm at Tring, an exclusively middle-class preserve, and came back cured of her stomach ulcers.

Chris was a sempstress at Worth's, and gave me tips about dressmaking: 'Always sew with silk thread,' she said. And I always have; it is worth the expense. She was small-boned, with quick, precise movements, and reminded me of the mice in Beatrix Potter's *The Tailor of Gloucester*, those industrious mice who sewed the button-holes of the tailor's embroidered waistcoat with cherry-coloured silk. Her biting wit was what delighted us. The Elmses used to tease us about idealizing "the workers" after the fashion of middle-class communists. 'The *workers*', Chris mocked me, 'the sods—they're no better than anyone else!' Mr Elms—we never got round to Christian names for their parents any more than we had done with the Watsons—drove a laundry van. He pronounced it "larndry" in the old-fashioned upper-class way, and had the self-effacing dignity which made the Elmses classless—class-conscious they were, but not class-ridden. Mrs Elms, who had been comely, still cared about her appearance; a new hat from the Co-op, paid for by her "divi", was a happy event. The Co-op paid their members a dividend based on what they bought, representing their share of the profits made by the Society.

To women of Mrs Elms's generation the Co-op signified fair trading and more. It was a political movement, an arm, like the TUC, of the Labour Party. I had to belong, though I didn't buy everything at the Co-op. Buying their goods I didn't mind; but belonging to the Co-op Guild was nothing like being friends with the Elmses. We met in the afternoon on a municipal housing estate. Under the Co-op insignia, a rainbow, we sang "Jerusalem" and began the meeting with a ritual called, I think, "praising". People would stand up and praise the Co-op goods. The younger Elmses—who never came to these meetings—would have stood up, as I longed to, and refuted the assertion that Co-op biscuits were best. Huntley and Palmer's were better. But I was not only class-ridden—and unsure of my own class—but fearfully bigoted, determined to carry out my new communist duties to the letter. Added to this was my wish to conform: it was like St Leonard's School all over again. In post-school life there is no handy set of rules to make or break you. But in the Communist Party there were restraints which suited me.

Had it not been for the Elmses my Party life in Barnes, contrasting, I sometimes complained, with James's political

Our honeymoon, 1934: 'The Wolseley Hornet bumped us across France at top speed'

Windrush, Inkpen, on the Berkshire Downs, 1935

Oswald Mosley leads a demonstration in London's East End, 1936:
'We joined the Communist Party'

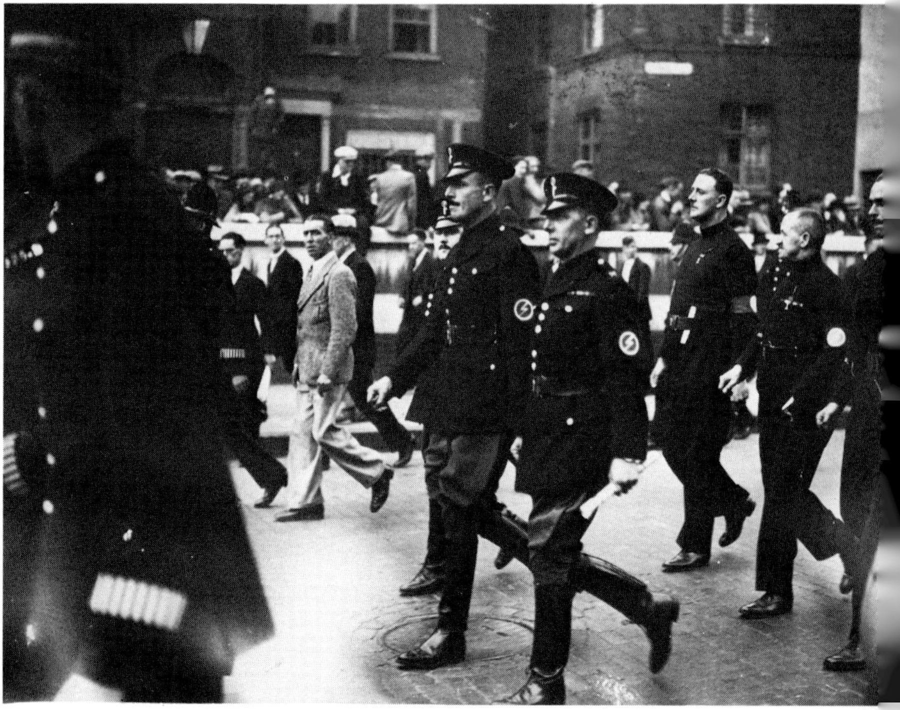

Jean Varda with his South Seas outrigger, Cassis, 1937. Roland Pym on left

Painting by Julian Trevelyan of the view from his studio

Left: Julian Trevelyan in his studio, Durham Wharf, Hammersmith, 1936

Right: My sister Ferelyth: 'She forged her own tools'

Varda's boat at Cassis: (*left to right*) Michael Higgins, Julian Trevelyan, Roland Pym, Joan Higgins

Left: With Janko Varda, Cassis 1936

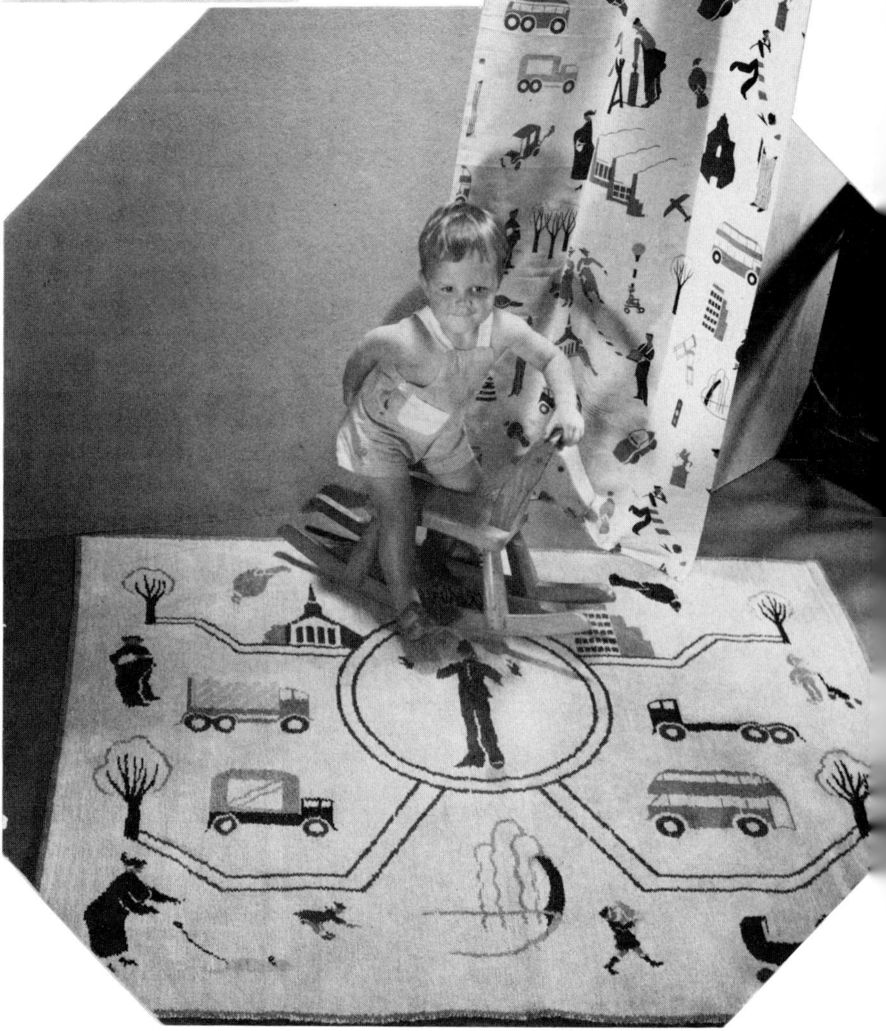

Hamish modelling for a Morton Sundour advertisement, 1938: 'All his toys were wooden and educational'

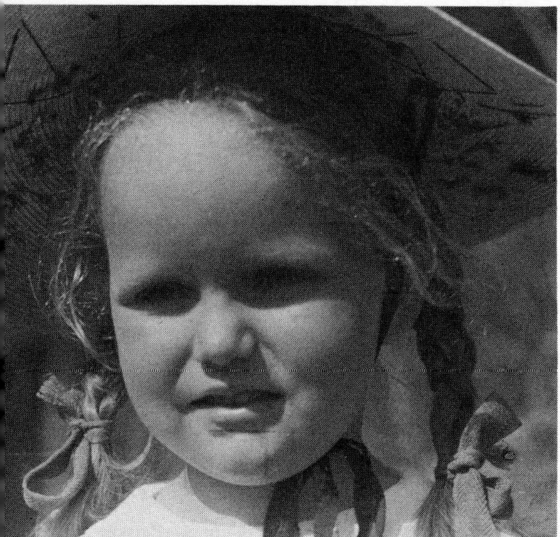

Above: May Day rally, London, 1938

Left: Janet at Abbey Farm, 1939

Right: Abbey Farm

Left: James on Manoeuvres

Right: With James fifty years later

lunches and activities in Bond Street and Soho, would have been tedious, limited to routine daily tasks delivering the *Worker*, pushing the Harrods pram with its Eric Gill initials round nearby housing estates, flipping copies from underneath Hamish's fur rug. Attending local meetings. *And reading the stuff.* "Literature" it was called. At branch meetings there was a "literature" table for pamphlets, booklets like Lenin's *Left-Wing Communism: An Infantile Disorder*, and publications like *Soviet Literature*. There were two obligatory handouts, the smudgier and less readable one called *Imprecor* (International Press Correspondence). I have forgotten the name of the other but both still stick in my gizzard.

At the Mechanic's Institute we were given a grounding in Marxist history, Moral Philosophy as well as Political and Economic Theory. Economic Theory was easiest, especially as I had imbibed Strachey's exposition. We had pictures to look at, though I found these distracting rather than helpful: there were wheatsheaves grasped by a proletarian fist; and something like a clock, or perhaps a cake that had been segmented but not cut. I could not attach correct meanings to these symbols, I would rather understand the theory in my head; the idea that a worker has nothing to exchange for subsistence except his labour is not difficult to grasp. He has nothing to lose but his chains—the illustration wasn't necessary.

The philosophy was a different matter. Marx abounds in Hegelian concepts which I seized on and made my own rather than taking them in as the speaker intended. '"The Interaction of Opposites",' I mused, 'that's James and me to the life.' There was another that became an enormous, expanding soap bubble. As for "The Negation of the Negation", it expressed black moods to a T.

After these lectures we went to a café for cups of strong tea and an informal meeting. Elsie Wintringham, Tom Wintringham's wife and a member of the Barnes C.P., sometimes joined us; and through her we heard news of Tom, a veteran soldier from World War I and commander of the British Battalion. During the battle of Jarama in February 1937 he was wounded and eventually invalided home. He and other brigadiers spoke in public to raise funds or recruit volunteers; but in private they said little. As I had learned as a child during World War I, when my uncle came home on leave with trench mud on his boots, soldiers don't talk much about their experiences. On the whole our talk was non-political, relaxed and rather sleepy. I generally found a seat next to Alf Cork, a burly, prosperous-looking plasterer with a considerate gallantry towards women. When Ribbentrop was made Hitler's London ambassador and ordered alterations at the German Embassy, Alf had adorned the false ceiling with a hidden hammer and sickle. I sat back, content to be accepted, bleary-eyed in the haze of cigarette smoke, steam and the smell of over-heated fat which permeated our clothing.

Accepted . . . If the Barnes C.P. was not exactly a substitute for the ideal family I was looking for, it provided a day-to-day structure with the monotony, the simple corporate duties attached to a family routine.

James did not attend these educational sessions—they weren't his idea of instructive entertainment. He was busy organizing various "Peace" committees, from the Peace Publicity Bureau, a small unit set up by the Artists' International Association, to the more official Arts Peace Campaign, comprising people of all views from Liberal leftwards. He brazenly had his Sundour office telephone number on the letter paper and his advertising work was frequently interrupted by urgent calls for posters and banners designed by the leading artists of the time. At meetings in King Street, Communist Party headquarters, directives were issued stressing the importance of gingering up the proliferating peace committees. The only subversive element was the constant drive to agitate for "Arms for Spain" (illegal under the Government's non-intervention policy), not just medical supplies. There was talk of "penetrating an organization and destroying it from within". But James was not in touch with anything that needed destroying (such as, at a guess, the Treasury, the armed forces, etc). An alternative was proposed: penetrating an organization to transform it. James may have helped to transform the Arts Peace Campaign. But I can't claim to have made many changes in the Barnes Co-op Women's Guild.

In the Barnes C.P. we intensified our local effort, the proliferation of Spanish Aid Committees, fund-raising, the campaign against the Government's non-intervention policy, meetings in drill halls and parish halls where the clergy—usually Methodist—were liberal enough to allow them.

James hired an excellent documentary film made by the Gas, Light and Coke Company showing bad housing compared with the flats they had built in Paddington to encourage the use of gas. In order to get the film James hastily made up a respectable title for himself: "Secretary of the Barnes and Mortlake Housing Association". The man from the gas company took him aside afterwards: 'We're not a communist organization,' he said, but he seemed more amused than shocked by the deception.

And there were open-air meetings at which James spoke with increasing enjoyment. He was trained at King Street by Ted Bramley, whose infallible system of headings on a postcard still served James when he became a practised speaker, part of his duties as an officer in the Intelligence Corps during World War II being to travel about lecturing the troops. His postcard system went with him everywhere, on to the first Camden Borough Council in 1964, when, as Labour Alderman, he became vice-Chairman of the Libraries and Arts Committee. Nowadays, watching him on the platform speaking to the Devon Historical Society, the Kingsbridge and District Ladies' Literary Guild, The Dawlish Women's Institute, it tickles me to imagine their reaction if they learnt the origins of the small cardboard oblong held in his hand!

Much has been written as to why middle-class people joined the Communist Party at the time. As for us, the Spanish Civil War cracked our shell at a crucial point in our encapsulated life, and laid us open to the poverty of the thirties, the state of near-starvation in which lower-paid workers, the unemployed and their families existed, which came to a head with the great Hunger Marches in 1931 and 1932. We knew about poverty in theory. Belonging to the Communist Party brought it home to us in a way which we could never otherwise have experienced. James had grown up close to an obscene degree of poverty. Glasgow Cathedral is not in a protected suburb like Golders Green. Children ran barefoot in Glasgow's bitterest weather. In St Andrew's I saw toddlers in winter sitting with bare buttocks on a granite kerb. A woman we knew, a widow with young children, applied for Assistance and was subjected to the Means Test. Her home was visited, her possessions turned over and she was advised to sell all but the bare necessities—a clock handed down from her grandmother, a chair that had belonged to her father, all went before she could claim supplementary benefits, as they are now called. Because it never occurred to us that society could be altered we grew up accepting it as it was. The Labour Party offered no dramatic solutions. But the Communist Party did. They promised a total re-structuring of society and showed us how it could be done. No country had succeeded in bringing about a transformation from capitalist to socialist society; but Russia, we believed, had gone a long way towards it. By 1936 dissentient voices, disillusioned accounts by travellers returning from the U.S.S.R., were increasing in volume and the great purges of 1936 and 1937 were widely reported, most fully by a press which had consistently shown itself hostile to the Russian Revolution and its consequences. Simply, we did not believe what we were told, or, as in the case of the execution of the generals, blindly accepted that their extinction was necessary. And the majority of our friends shared our view, or, as time went on, ceased to be our friends. One exception was John Pattisson, who may have enjoyed pricking our holier-than-thou priggishness. Working at Secker and Warburg he seemed to be in a nest of Trotskyists. Trotskyists emerged as our worst enemies. Apart from their political heresy they were a local nuisance: their theory was unshakeable but they argued interminably; and in practical work their argumentativeness made them so inefficient that they appeared to be saboteurs.

Our experience in Barnes was very different from that of the academics at Oxford and Cambridge. Not for us the discussions, thrashing out of differences, dramatic decisions followed by breast-beating recantations. At the time I am writing about, and for years to come, we never discussed anything: we acted.

Our subsequent behaviour was full of inconsistencies, absurdities and on my part an obtuse callousness, specially towards my mother. All of which arose from our characters and cannot be blamed on the Party.

Idealistic we were; but not, I think, beyond what the promise of a foreseeable future justified. We were living through a bad, hard, gritty time. I never felt certain we should win. No-one we knew would have echoed Wordsworth's words:

> Bliss was it in that dawn to be alive;
> And to be young was very Heaven!

Rather it was Auden who expressed what we felt:

> Some possible dream, long coiled in the ammonite's slumber
> Is uncurling, prepared to lay on our talk and our kindness
> Its military silence, its surgeon's idea of pain.
>
> And out of the Future into actual History,
> As when Merlin, tamer of horses, and his lords to whom
> Stonehenge was still a thought, the Pillars passed
>
> And into the undared ocean swung north their prow,
> Drives through the night and star-concealing dawn
> For the virgin roadsteads of our hearts an unwavering keel.

W. H. Auden, and to a lesser extent Stephen Spender and their fellow poets, were a greater source of inspiration for me than anything else I read or heard during the years that preceded World War II, with the possible exception of Professor J. B. S. Haldane who, through his popular scientific writing linked with Marxist theory, gave us sounder-based, more lasting belief that society could be changed by socialism. Sounder, I mean, than we got from our potted communist theory, and this, as much as anything, from the persuasive force of his character and bearing, and the practical demonstrations of his beliefs through his work.

XIII
Julian Trevelyan and Durham Wharf

OUR LIFE IN Barnes wasn't all pamphlets, banners and party meetings. A very different world awaited us over the river. Not long after our arrival at Riverview Gardens Joan Higgins gave us an introduction to Julian Trevelyan, the painter, who lived in Hammersmith. I rang up and he answered—why not come this afternoon?

Somehow I had got the idea that Julian was a picture-framer as well as a painter. So I took with me in the pram the reproduction of a painting by Bauer which James had brought back from Germany, austere, black and white like a Plimsoll mark on a ship's side.

Hamish and I sped across Hammersmith Bridge—the pram pushed perfectly, walking was easier with than without it—and worked our way along the further bank between high corrugated walls where building was in slow progress, over puddles and wet clay, past a pub called The Doves, past the solidly built water-pumping station, and came out in Hammersmith Terrace where I knew A. P. Herbert, "a famous author", lived—all I knew about him then was that he had written *The Water Gypsies*.

Durham Wharf is at the far end. We halted at a blue door in the wall. The Trevelyans ran a picture library. And through the shop window to the right a small unappealing painting of a blue frog on a green ground (by Max Ernst, it turned out) caught my attention as the door was opened by a very tall man with a shock of dark hair and strange, unforgettable features. Today Julian wears a beard cut to follow the line of his jaw; his head is like a piece of Greek sculpture. But I think then his face appeared a little out of balance, perhaps because of his unruly hair and teeth. Julian is roughly James's age. But he seemed more grown-up. He already had a world of experience behind him from his life in Paris learning to paint.

And he is a Trevelyan, as Ursula, his first wife, is a Darwin, both part of a network of great, interrelated families (Ursula's great-grandfather was Charles Darwin). Their heredity gave them, by nature and nurture, a grounding of experience, an unconsciously authoritative bearing which awed and attracted me, at our first meeting, not quite comfortably. It took time before I was at ease in Julian's company.

That first day, leaving Hamish asleep in a small walled garden, and having disposed of the Bauer reproduction—Julian with restrained politeness explained that he didn't frame pictures himself but could have it done—we stepped over the sill of a stable door into an enormous studio filled with light, cold light from the north panes in the roof, and dancing river light from a window that stretched from wall to wall. The tide was full; swans sailed by, a dinghy rocked at anchor.

The walls were covered with paintings and drawings; an early, oblong piano that Chopin might have used stood on a raised floor. There were too many curious, striking objects to take in all at once. The effect was one of intense aliveness and awareness as though the room itself was alive, a disturbing sensation. One thing stood out: hanging on the wall was a clean, new aluminium frying pan with a plaster poached egg on it. I was at first knocked for six, then distinctly put out, as no doubt the Surrealists intended. (Their exhibition in New Burlington Gardens had just closed. James said the object which made him feel most creepy was a fur cup and saucer.)

Even now, when I detect my lazy mind closing up to new ideas, I remind myself of the poached egg.

I was in any case prepared for something shocking. I had never before been in a room used for sleeping and eating. The ample double bed in one corner reminded me of my mother's suspicion that all writers and painters are amoral, and that painters are the worst. Time passed, several parties, before I gave up my fantasy of undefined orgies, a general laxity resulting from not having any proper work to do ("Proper work" meant going to an office every day.) Then I observed that Julian and Ursula, a potter, worked hard and methodically in their separate studios. Another thing that impressed me was the way Julian and his friends would sit talking after breakfast and then go off to work all day without an office routine to compel them.

Rich as the thirties were in experimental and social movements, Julian seemed to be involved in them all, including Mass Observation. His territory at one time was North-West England and in addition to observing people in pubs, shops and wherever they happened to be he painted them. His paintings done in Whitehaven, a coastal port, marked a new phase in his work. We thought of it as his "tombstone" period, there seemed to be so many studies of churchyards. And he was experimenting with collages, an unsuitable medium for the purpose: 'Bits of newspaper blew all over the street.' Julian himself wrote what has been acknowledged by the founders of the movement to be the best and most entertaining account of Mass Observation in his autobiographical book, *Indigo Days*, published by James at MacGibbon and Kee in 1957.

When you have lived a lifetime with someone it is not always easy to distinguish opinions formed together, events shared, from ideas separately arrived at, events vicariously experienced. So it is with memories of Durham Wharf.

'Durham Wharf,' says James, 'was a clearing house for anyone interested in the arts. Anyone from abroad, if he was lucky, bore an introduction to Julian.' Though this sounds like a main-line railway station, it does describe the feeling one sometimes got from the place, specially at parties, which James went to more often than I. Julian's parties were to me like medieval battlefields, trampling armies brilliantly emblazoned, from which, a foot soldier, one emerged without honour or profit, yet with a cathartic clear-headedness, as after strenuous games-playing. Walking home by the river, picking our way among puddles reflecting the London sky, James would tell me the names of the famous people he had recognized, met, spoken to. Auden, Spender, MacNeice—perhaps because I had by then begun seriously to write, I should not have wanted to meet them, my companions in thought, my mentors, lighting me through those dark days. I shouldn't have known what to say to them. My aloofness at parties may have been partly to do with the fact that, surprising as it now seems, I didn't drink much.

Boat Race parties were the best, studio and garden packed with people in spring clothes, children and dogs pushing between our legs, a great spring festival, the river *en fête*, the roar from thousands of throats as the boats neared us, the whistling and baying of boats and tugs, hooters, a crescendo of cheering as the oarsmen came into view. And what a moment that was! So frail, so small their craft, passing as it seemed slowly yet briefly across our vision, strained thighs moving like pistons, shoulders already bowed by anguish and exhaustion (for the race was said to be won or lost between Hammersmith Bridge and Chiswick Eyot), how could one not weep seeing these young heroes striving to be matched with their hour?

'People,' James says, 'came as much for the fun of the food and drink, of seeing friends, as for the race.' I came for the race.

The people I remember were those to be found there when the studio was almost empty, the paintings and objects most alive: Sandy Calder's great mobile suspended from the rafters flanked by a globular, dried, puffed-out fish like a giant sea-hedgehog, African masks, a piece of African sculpture on the bookshelves running the length of the river window, the pot-stove, the cats—all familiar, no longer strange or disturbing. A girl stands by the window, her fair hair greenish in the watery light. She is from Normandy, and often comes to stay, drawing out with her serenity the timeless quality of the place, its unity in diversity. On the sofa Len Lye, the avant-garde film director, talks about jazz with Roland Pym, the painter; Len's young son, named Bix after the trumpeter Bix Beiderbecke, sits on his knee. A Polish painter is there, staying for weeks on end. Humphrey Jennings, whose work in a new genre, film documentaries, appealed to my liking for whatever is compressed, inferential rather than exhaustively detailed, had just done a documentary for the GPO Film Unit, *Night Mail*, with words by W. H. Auden, music by Benjamin Britten. Humphrey Jennings had his own version of Mass Observation. He wanted to "touch the Unconscious of the working classes". A small, quiet brown man was often there—Tambimuttu, who started *Poetry London*, introducing me to new poets I had never heard of, like David Gascoigne.

Ralph Parker, whom we had come to know at the Higginses, turned out to be an old friend of Julian's, often to be found at Durham Wharf. The Trevelyans and the Higginses were having dinner with us on 30 November 1936, when the telephone rang and I answered it. 'Mr Parker,' I reported, jibbing as always at using Christian names, 'says the Crystal Palace is on fire.' Off they went, laughing all the way down the stairs at my flat, formal announcement. I had an additional basically snobbish reason for not coming out with "Ralph": I'd failed to hear on the phone if he was still "Rafe" or if, like other middle-class comrades, he'd changed his pronunciation to suit the Party.

At Durham Wharf we met those who were to become lasting friends: Jean Varda, the Greek painter, and the Herbert family, above all Jocelyn. Before her marriage to Anthony Lousada, who combined painting with being a solicitor, she had begun her career as stage designer in which she was to become pre-eminent. Their honeymoon in Paris, Anthony complained, had to be cut short so that she could come back to her work for the left-wing Unity Theatre.

And there was Michael Wickham who with Tanya, a girl he was to marry, lived for a while at Durham Wharf. Michael is probably best known as a photographer, though I still think of him as a painter, one of many accomplishments—too many. I've always been a sucker for people who "tell me things"; Michael expects you to know as much as he does. He would pull a volume of Saint-Simon's memoirs from the poacher's-pocket of his corduroy velvet jacket supposing you to be as familiar as he with eighteenth-century life and literature. He might break into French with a regional accent—he and Paul Valéry could have conversed in Niçoise. Michael was dark with an ivory skin, his hair worn longish, his bone structure almost Mongolian. He was interested in everything, did too many things equally well, perfecting whatever he turned his hand to, leaving in his wake handsome furniture, guitars, lutes, gardens, houses restored around and over the heads of his growing family—for his several wives always wanted, understandably, to replicate their talented husband. Renewed ingenuities and skills were forever brought into play for what he did with such care did not pay well enough. Michael had learned Russian so as to be able to read the great nineteenth-century writers in the original. He, alone among our communist friends, had mastered Marxist theory, read Kropotkin, Bakunin, studied the background to the Russian Revolution.

Wit and laughter are the hardest qualities to bring alive in writing. Michael clowned like the best of French clowns, Marcel Marceau, in Michael's case using mime and gesture to evoke pleasurable lewdness. Watching students of today's theatre eschewing symbolism in favour of attempted realism, simulating copulation etc. on the stage, I thought they should have seen what Michael could do with a Maison Pearson hairbrush!

So, on the south bank there was the C.P., gusty, gritty winds, bird-haunted reservoirs and long walks with Party "literature" under Hamish's pram cover. And across the river was Julian's world, equally active in Spain's support, the talents of writers, painters, musicians transforming our routine propaganda. The Surrealist Group, in which Julian was a leading figure, were the most effective, satirizing with their irrationality the irrational folly of our rulers.

One event did most fully and enjoyably bring us all together. The May Day march of 1937 was a great Popular Front demonstration, a real May Day holiday, hot enough for women to wear summer frocks. The prettiest girl on the march was Jocelyn Herbert, then about nineteen; she wore a muslin dress and carried a large Winterhalter straw hat. Her fiancé, Anthony Lousada, on view for the first time, joined her as we neared Hyde Park. Looking back and forward, the four-abreast column seemed endless. The route from Charing Cross was prepared for George VI's coronation and the flags and decorations waved in happy counterpoint against richly decorated trades union banners, the scarlet communist and trades council banners. Beside me walked my cousin, Peggy Hamilton, from New Zealand, and her father, George Wills, a fiercely radical Liberal who would have liked to blow up Londonderry House—he had a particular hatred for his lordship whose right-wing views on Spain were already making him a target for all anti-fascist groups.

Our slogans were peaceable: 'Butter not guns!' From behind

us Philip Toynbee could be heard intoning his own version of the advertisement for Horlick's Malted Milk: 'Masturbation not night starvation!' (Not approved, needless to say, by the Party). I walked beside Alf Cork, our master plasterer friend. He and I knew all the words of the "Internationale": 'On our flesh has battened long the raven,' we sang (Alf was amply proportioned), 'Too long we've been the vulture's prey!' The verses, as opposed to the tune, seemed to me a ludicrous translation of a fine marching song and I once said so in front of Alan Bush, the composer, who turned on me fiercely, his beaky profile like a bird of prey, a noble hawk or eagle, as he recited them with passion, convincing me of their essential truth. In any case, as it had become the battle hymn of our comrades in Spain, this was no time for mealy-minded criticism. 'Then comrades come rally,' we sang, passing Grosvenor House, 'The last fight let us face, the Internationale unites the human race!' It was possible on that day, as part of that enormous concourse, to believe that it did. Ahead of us in Hyde Park scarlet banners were already catching the sunlight, winding among the light spring leaves.

From time to time a sharpish breeze blew up, and Alf took off his scarf and wound it round my neck. He glanced behind us at a contingent of Oxford students in their gowns. 'It's good to see the lady comrades out,' he remarked, 'but it's a pity one of them has egg down her front.' The Party were very hot on our being well turned-out.

When we had dispersed in the park and were gathered together for tea, the Higginses introduced us to the egg-stained comrade. She was Ianthe Elstob, and her mother struck me as going a bit far in her energetic recommendations to her daughter to get into bed with men as often and as freely as possible. I realize now that her mother's talk was typical of emancipated women of her generation and that Ianthe was unlikely to have been put out by her mother's teasing: at the time I thought it might put her off sex for life. It was unnecessary anyway, for Ianthe, the only girl I have ever met outside fiction to have violet eyes, was soon to marry John Carswell, the writer, for good. Almost exactly twenty years after that May Day march, Ianthe and Peggy Duff were to be the first to start a peace movement which, by 1958, had become the Campaign for Nuclear Disarmament.

We had reason to feel hopeful, that May afternoon. News from Spain was encouraging; Madrid still held out. In February the Battle of the Jarama and more decisively the Republican victory at Guadalajara in March had relieved, though it did not end the siege, as Franco and his German and Italian allies turned their attention to the North and the Basque campaign.

About that time there had been a naval engagement between a Nationalist cruiser and a merchant ship carrying arms for the Republicans in Bilbao. Three Basque trawlers were shot to pieces fighting the cruiser.

This caught my imagination because it was a sea-battle, but more permanently because of C. Day Lewis's poem about it.

Freedom is more than a word, more than the base coinage
Of statesmen, the tyrant's dishonoured cheque, or the dreamer's mad
Inflated currency. She is mortal, we know, and made
In the image of simple men who have no taste for carnage
But sooner kill and are killed than see that image betrayed.

This is what I mean by saying that we were caught up in great events, movements deeply felt rather than analysed.

How did these great movements affect Hamish and me as we whipped across Hammersmith Bridge, gulls crying in the iron rigging, making for Palmer's Stores, the Co-op or the market? Or sitting in Margaret Elms' tiny living room drinking tea with the comrades while Hamish and Donald played around our feet? (Each of us rinsed our own cup in cold water and turned it upside down on the draining board.)

My pervading memory is of a growing stress under a burden of responsibility for world events which we could not influence—though we thought we should, or ought to try, all the more because in socialism we held the key to end poverty, misery, war itself. The stress was like an illness. The pain of Guernica was a bodily pain, one with the pain of weaning.

Nowadays they tell me that the process of weaning is no

longer traumatic, being allowed to happen naturally. Then it was done by the book, taking six weeks, ending with Epsom salts and strapped breasts when the child was nine months old—though no other mother I knew carried on so long. Hamish seemed to survive the trauma. But I continued unwell and in June we left Hamish with my parents and went to stay with Jean Varda, the painter, in Cassis.

Janko, as he was called, was a Greek, dark, compact, with palpable physical strength, and the air of releasing slow, controlled energy from every pore of his squarely proportioned body. He walked as though spring-heeled; and seemed continuously, quietly amused with life, never more so than when telling stories about his childhood on a Greek island.

'My mother was a seal,' he said at the outset of one of his long, winding tales, and we envisaged him surfacing on to a rocky ledge, water streaming off his straight-fringed, round-cropped head. His hair was iron-grey by the time we knew him, but though older than us his vitality made him ageless. He loved women; and never lived alone. He appeared to have no money and to need none. At supper we ate a dish of beans, oil, lemon juice, garlic and fresh herbs, familiar now but then part of his story-telling.

Janko had begun to make a new kind of mosaic, fragments of plate-glass mirror embedded in cement, parts of the picture painted over. We bought one of a Greek island with a lighthouse and hung it in our sitting room where the glass pieces reflected the river light. Wherever we have lived since we have found a place where the picture could catch the light, the island with water forever in movement running past its precipitous grey and yellow cliffs and cliff-hanging houses—a yellow like the cover of the Albatross edition of *To The Lighthouse*, read for the first time in my cabin on the way to Africa, with water-refracted light moving over the white painted bulkhead.

In summer Janko lived in Cassis in an unfurnished house lent him by friends. This year, the summer of 1937, Tanya Wickham was staying with him. They had hired or borrowed essential furniture. The house was enormous, high-ceilinged. Our room, with its long window overlooking a cherry orchard, held a bosomy French bed with curly wire ends, a Van Gogh chair and a table. The cool grey walls were decorated with a "wallpaper" of real crimson clove carnations. We ate that night, and every succeeding day and night in unchanging weather, under cherry trees hung with fruit, moths banging softly about the oil lamp on the table, lit when the Mediterranean light gave way to mothlike dusk. Everything, I noticed dubiously that first evening, was left on the table when we went to bed, washing ourselves in a volcano-shaped basin set in handmade ceramic tiles. There would be a mess to clear up in the morning, I reflected, sinking into the feather bed.

But in the morning there was the table under the cherries, the checked cloth laid for breakfast, a smell of coffee and hot rolls in the kitchen where Tanya was sweeping the floor with a Cinderella broom, like a Russian peasant in her full-skirted gingham. She had a great Russian smile, Tanya, and was altogether not unlike a Russian sunflower.

Still convalescent, I did not often leave the garden but lay mostly in the shade. Or wrote in my notebook.

James went sailing with the others in a half-decked, clinker-built fishing boat; Janko had set Tanya and me to repair the main sail with a curved needle and a sailor's palm. They caught sardines and Janko grilled them wrapped in fennel and garlic on an iron grid over a pit of glowing olive ash.

The day we left we went to lunch with friends of Janko's noted for their vegetarian cooking. The variety of vegetables and the subtlety of their preparation made this one of two unforgettable meals on that holiday. The other was in Avignon where we broke our journey home. James took me to a restaurant for our last dinner on a terrace overlooking the river. The full moon, a little misted, cast a blue light over all. The exquisite plainness of what we ate—grilled trout fresh from a tank, chicken with a lemon sauce, cheese and cherries, and Pouilly Fuissé—all was so exactly to my taste that the dinner has remained in memory as it was when we ate it.

In the train that night I felt a sense of fulfilment, of uncommon well-being. I was pregnant; and when we learnt this it seemed a natural culmination of our time in Cassis.

We stopped off in Paris to see the International Exhibition initiated by the Popular Front government. There were the

Russian and German pavilions confronting one another, on the one hand two comrades striding forward with hammer and sickle, on the other a giant Nazi emblem over the legend, "Strength through Joy", both cast in concrete, equally monolithic, with a startling similarity. In the Spanish pavilion Picasso's "Guernica" was on view for the first time.

On our return we went straight down to Barton-on-Sea where my parents had a holiday house. Hamish was sitting up in his carry-cot, so grown, so brown, so changed that I felt a pang of jealousy, of loss at having been deprived of those two weeks with him. As we carried him up to his bath I vowed never to leave him again.

XIV

The Basque Home; the End of the Spanish Civil War

IMMEDIATELY ON OUR return, in June 1937, we were plunged into preparations for the Basque Children's Home. The story of the bombing of Guernica and other Basque towns by German planes is too well-known to need re-telling. The whole of the Western world was shocked by the systematic destruction of open towns, the slaughter of civilians. For many it was the turning-point, bringing them into active support of the Republicans. By the beginning of May four thousand children had been crowded into the *Habana*, a liner owned by the Basque Government, brought to England and encamped at North Stonham in Hampshire.

We took on as many as would fill a large house in Putney. "We" being an all-Party, strictly non-political committee set up under the chairmanship of Stephan Hopkinson, then curate of Saint John's Church on Putney Hill. If anything could get me into the Church of England it would be Stephan, whose scholarly intellect, humour and affection for humankind were given sharper definition by his attractive dark wife, Anne. She had given up her career as a singer at Sadler's Wells to marry him and bring up a large family, and was outspokenly left-wing. Anne and Stephan were natural friends, or would have been had our exertions given us a let-up for the friendship which we resumed in less fraught times. They were as young as we were and I think Stephan's assistant, Chad Varah, must have been even younger. He was thought, or so I remember, to be something of a clerical tearaway, an *enfant terrible* with the ladies on parish outings. He certainly enlivened our task with his gift for seeing what wanted doing and his original way of solving problems, and it was no surprise to hear, after the War, that he had founded The Samaritans.

Lady Layton was on the committee, she who had led us at the Hall School on United Nations Day, presumably representing the Liberal Party, now lending authority with her tactful presiding presence. There was a Labour Party member whose daughter volunteered to become resident House Mother. And a lively, forceful Jewish tailor, adept at fund-raising—all in all, Stephan got together a group which promised to work well with the minimum of discussion. I can't recall anything about the Trotskyist referred to earlier as an argumentative nuisance; and I am the last person to complain since, in my limited experience of committee work, I was soon found to be talking too much, seizing on irrelevant points, chasing hares of my own, and finding myself at loggerheads with at least one co-member. In this case it was the girl who became House Mother. We crossed swords so often that at last I determined on a showdown at the next committee meeting. To intimidate her I decided on the extreme measure of wearing a hat, not normally worn by our members. When I turned up she was wearing one too!

But first the house, in poor shape, had to be got ready. Frank Paterson, scrubbing floors, said that after his (honourable) stretch in prison he had sworn never to scrub another floor. Only his friendship with James got him back on his knees. With his expertise he showed James how it should be done, working with the grain and drying every section quickly. As they worked away he ironically remarked, à propos of Stalin's increasing prominence, 'We're going in for the personality cult.' As with Jewish and anti-Catholic jokes, it would have been dicey for recent communist converts like us to crack anti-communist jokes. James and I would not have joked about Stalin whom we thought of as "Uncle Jo", an august, watchful parent. But established members were free enough with their criticism, and not the deadly humourless individuals they are sometimes made out to be. When Victor Gollancz was about to publish a certain Left Book Club choice Harry Pollitt begged him not to: 'I've enough trouble on my hands as it is what with the old man, the long bugger and that bloo-ody red arse of a dean!' (Referring to Stalin, Palme Dutt and Hewlett Johnson, Dean of Canterbury).

In June the Basque children tumbled out of the coach that brought them to Putney, all dark, vigorous, with prune-coloured eyes. They ranged from about three to fourteen and I hardly learned to distinguish one from another.

These children had been exposed to traumatic experiences which, today, are the lot of a majority of the world's children. At that time the full terrible truth of what had happened to them was new, at least to us. Their bearing was phenomenal. They were Basques with the stubborn pride of their independent people. Their country had been overrun but not yet conquered. This they knew, even the youngest. When the fall of Bilbao, their capital, was announced while they were encamped they stoned the bringers of bad news: some went wild with grief and ran away from the camp.

We "adopted" two, not to live with us but to "have an interest taken in them." Ramirez was about twelve, his sister, Nievis, was younger. Their elder sister was among a group who had come to England to help with the children. These two were not originally with the Putney contingent, and it is typical of our arrogance that we more or less dragooned Ferelyth into fetching them from North London in Daddy's Austin. They were sick all the way and it's typical of her resourcefulness that she stopped at an Express Dairy for a dozen empty milk cartons to save what was still unsullied of the Austin's back seat. Ferelyth wasn't often irate but this time she was, having Daddy to face on her return.

My sister whom, when we were children, I had thought of as the archetypal girl, gentle, easily moved to compassionate tears, had turned out to be an adventurous traveller, a crack rider on a dude ranch in America, a sculptor who forged her own tools, an innovator at the Central School of Art where she wrested from copper rod a life-size gibbon monkey that hung there in the staircase well. During the war, when she was in the W.R.N.S. servicing radios for the Fleet Air Arm, she married our cousin, Bill Wills, a bomber pilot. Together they became proficient gliders. She could come out very strong on anything she felt deeply about.

We were in the bathroom in Hampstead when I sounded off on what must have by then become for the family a stick-in-the-groove gramophone record. 'Don't you *mind* about Germany,' I cried, 'the Jews, the concentration camps?' 'It's the Chinese I mind more about,' she replied. We worried about the Chinese people too. We knew about their epic fight against Chiang Kai-Shek and the Japanese invaders from Edgar Snow's book about the Long March, *Red Star Over China*, a Left Book Club choice, and from a meeting at the Earls Court stadium addressed by the Dean of Canterbury, "The Red Dean", on his return from China. They were part of the world to be saved: but they were so far away. Ferelyth loved them for themselves, for their arts and their ancient civilization.

Soon we had a car of our own, a Morris van of a new design with the driver's seat over the engine and a sliding door. An aunt of James's had left him some money and, after giving a donation to the Party and a lump sum and a rise to Edith as a comradely gesture, we bought the van because it would be useful for Party work. It held nine guildswomen and (separately) at least nineteen Basque children plus Hamish in his carry-cot. Away we went, Hamish and I and the Basques, to the local swimming baths, kitted out with swimsuits which they had to be got into tactfully for even the smallest were extremely modest by our standards and wouldn't expose themselves naked. Intrepid, reckless, mostly unable to swim, they all jumped into the deep end and I, round-bellied, jumped in after them. They were all fished out unharmed. Physically nothing affected them. The doctors who examined them remarked on their health, putting down their immunity from infection to the tomatoes and oranges and olive oil and garlic they had lived on, and still did. A Spanish chef had turned up at the outset in a spotless white overall and tall hat, masterful as all good chefs are said to be, and more or less took over the Home.

'They need very much food,' he told us. 'Plate piled so high a dog can't jump over it.' (A Spanish saying.)

Our worst crisis was caused by his not getting on with the girl who was ostensibly in charge, with a young man to help her, an unenviable task in that bare-boarded ill-lit house with its institutional smell only alleviated by Spanish cooking smells from the kitchen. There was something unappetizing about those two, I used to think, about their paleness, her flakey skin, his nonentity, though I couldn't withhold my respect for their sticking to their posts.

Not surprisingly they found a way of alleviating their hard lives. It was the chef who first complained that they were sleeping together. Whether because of the straitlaced conventions of the time, or because of his personal dislike, he made an issue of this and it had to be seriously taken up. At a Committee meeting the chef made the most of what he described as scenes of licentious debauchery between the shameless pair. 'These things are all over the place,' he cried, and blew his cheeks out, 'in the house, in the garden—the children are *blowing them up like balloons*!' And he cast a French letter on the table before Lady Layton. She, with true Liberal impartiality, took the girl's side. I didn't, from prejudice against the girl, not from morality. If, as I think, they had to go, it can't have been easy to replace them.

Mother and Ferelyth came to our Christmas party. First there was an English tea and English games amid English paper-chains and Spanish posters including the famous one of a bare foot and the words "*No pasaran!*" ("They shall not pass") which had become the symbol of Spanish resistance. Then the children sang their own songs, danced their own dances. At the end they sang "The Internationale" with raised arms, clenched fists. These children were not, for the most part, communists. The song had become their anthem. Sung by them in that setting, a song which has since been cheapened, misappropriated, held then its full true meaning.

The summer of 1937 was clouded by the perpetual nausea of my pregnancy, very different from Hamish's beginning. We took the Basque children for picnics to Kew and to Chiswick Park. When I drive past the gates today that Palladian dome, those layered cedars are still overcast for me with an oily film of yellowish light. Physical malaise was bound up with the news of what was happening in Spain. The Battle of Brunete, in the autumn of 1937, was a Pyrrhic victory: the International

Brigade suffered severe losses. When a Brigader whom we knew or knew by reputation, perhaps younger than ourselves, was killed or wounded, the news was the more shocking. John Cornford, the first Englishman to go to Spain in 1936, was killed in December 1937, the day after his twenty-first birthday. A Party friend described how he had come back to England to recruit volunteers, had visited her Young Communist camp and admonished her and her fellow-students for enjoying themselves so uninhibitedly at this time of crisis. The poem he wrote to Margot Heinemann before the Battle of Brunete was added to my anthology. I was still young enough to learn by heart easily and keep in mind what I learnt.

Julian Bell, Virginia Woolf's nephew, was killed driving an ambulance in July 1937. He belonged to the first medical unit to go to Spain shortly after the outbreak of war, organized by Kenneth Loutitt, a medical student on the point of taking his Finals at Bart's. His story shows the courage, the bold, practical improvisation needed at the time. He assembled a contingent of nurses and doctors, none over thirty, and the makings of a field hospital, a portable operating table, an ambulance, drugs and dressings. Kenneth himself was a romantic figure, dark-haired with sallow pockmarked skin; his deep-set black eyes had a searching look often seen in Spanish paintings. When we first met him in London in 1943 he was dressed, as he must have been in Spain, in a dust-covered leather jerkin. He had come from rescuing the living and disinterring the dead after an air raid. He described the conditions they had found when they got out to Spain. Almost all the army doctors had deserted to Franco's side. There were almost no drugs or supplies of any kind and soon they were short of the simplest needs, even soap. New treatments had to be devised. Whenever possible wounds were left open and exposed to sunlight. Some of these new techniques were used during World War II.

But our perambulations—Hamish's and mine—about the Castlenau estates, and my routine duties at the Basque Home, were not all clouded by empty depression over-ridden by souped-up political fervour. There was occasional theatregoing, to the communist-run Unity Theatre where a number of actresses, actors and directors made their début, including Alfie Bass and Ted, now Lord Willis. In their Christmas pantomime, "Babes in the Wood", Vida Hope played Neville Chamberlain as Fairy Godmother with an impotent wand that always drooped at critical moments. And we saw most of the Group Theatre productions directed by Rupert Doone. Auden's *The Ascent of F6* struck home, for it was about his mother, shrouded, isolated on a mountain peak; guilt feelings about my own mother were never far from the surface. Most influential of all were the Russian films directed by Eisenstein and Pudovkin. *Battleship Potemkin*, the Czar's soldiers advancing down the long flight of steps, the shooting, the wicker pram left bumping down from step to step. Who can forget the scene on the ice in *Ivan The Terrible*, with Prokofiev's music, the sinister hooded ecclesiastical knights routed on the frozen river? Or the bare foot of the cleaner polishing the corridor on the train in *Storm over Asia*, symbolizing the slave life of the peasants under Czarism more effectively than any propagandist realism could have done?

And there were socials and dances organized by James and the Arts Peace Campaign. At the best of these, run by the Artists' International Association, the singer, Hedli Anderson, Louis MacNeice's wife, sang cabaret songs written by Auden with music by Benjamin Britten. "I'm a jam tart" and "Tell me the truth about love" became family songs.

Hamish, who had a good ear and at six months could sing the opening bars of "Heilige Nacht", as the wooden angels on Mother's Austrian musical box slowly rotated, was weaned on songs from Kurt Weill's *Drei Groschen Oper*, on Marlene Dietrich singing "Johnny", on Cole Porter, Jerome Kern, and Ella Fitzgerald singing "I lost my yellow basket". And the flat resounded with tunes from the Fred Astaire films that came to Hammersmith. "And it really doesn't matter if the rain goes pitter-patter," we sang dancing down the long corridor that led to the river room with Hamish after us. And "Let's call the whole thing off. . . But oh! if we had to call the whole thing off then we must part, and oh!—if we had to part then that might break my heart!"

How unlikely that seemed then! Yet we were already to a

degree separated by our political involvement that kept James "over the river" more and more often. Constrained as we were by hard, urgent stress, even James looked stern. I was no longer living with my hand in his pocket as in that far-off evening outside the walls of Wormwood Scrubs; had I given thought to it, life without his constant protection was chill, as though I had a skin too few. We were living in a bad time for lovers, for husbands and wives.

For James, life was to be lived in the present; he embraced experience as he had swallowed bananas whole on our romantic Austrian journey. Planning for the future made him feel ill; solicitors, insurance men were to be avoided at all cost. What he most disliked about my father was his being a chartered accountant with all that implied as to the petty reckoning and conservation of financial resources. Whereas I suspect that I was already beginning to miss, and to try to recreate in myself, the very characteristics I had spurned in marrying a man as unlike my father as possible.

At the same time, while outwardly active, one effect of my being in the Party was to encourage an inward retreat: true feeling was replaced by a simulacrum of normal behaviour, a shaky defence against anxiety which was to carry me through the war years till, with the coming of peace, I collapsed. Trying to be a member of the Communist Party, like being at St Leonard's, favoured the growth of mental disorder, while by contrast being at the Hall School made for true feeling, common sense, sanity. Albeit unconsciously, James was hurt and baffled by my withdrawal, all the more because he is not one for abstract reflection. While outwardly his loving self, he responded with an inner hardening, growing his own shell.

Before the new baby's arrival Edith left to get married. Dear Edith! From the beginning she had been there, with her red-gold hair, her wide smile, her cyclist's calves, seen us change, suffered my moods and inconsistencies. She "came along with us" though we never enquired into her political views. We assumed that she was "with us". She even consented to appear on the platform in the Conway Hall at a meeting to discuss the formation of a Domestic Servants' Union, and spoke shortly and to the point—after the chairman had announced that her employers had given her the afternoon off for the occasion, at which the audience clapped!

To replace Edith I went to a hotel off Great Russell Street where German refugees were herded together, waiting to be hired. They were seated on gold chairs in what might have been a ballroom, many of them elderly women in fur coats, some with swollen ankles overbrimming neat shoes or button boots, those ankles patiently crossed, like their wrists on their laps. They didn't look as though they had ever worked, or could hope to work. Their faces were masked by an impenetrable weariness. Swallowing my shame, I chose a young strong girl with pebble glasses called Lotte.

That night we sat as usual in the draughty kitchen with its pulley hung with nappies, its canyon glimpse of the river between walls, listening to "Monday Night at Eight", a nice, non-political radio show with Gert and Daisy, Valentine Dyall as "The Man in Black" and Arthur Askey singing about his "busy, busy bee". The news followed. Hitler and Mussolini had met; Austria was threatened. By now our Government with their comings and goings between the Axis power seemed to us totally impotent, criminally irresponsible, and the Labour opposition worse since they might have been supposed to know better. The Popular Front movement seemed powerless to sway the mass of the people. We began to see that there was little hope of help for Spain, none of converting the British to socialism before the whole of Europe was engulfed in war.

Our daughter Janet was born on 14 March 1938, the day Hitler marched into Austria. But of that I knew nothing. Spring had come early, almond blossom was fully out, the sky a cloudless blue. However tired you may have been, a miraculous strength comes over you when a baby is ready to be born, an expectant joy, restless yet with an inner calm.

I refused chloroform because working-class women were not given it—a futile gesture. But it was, nevertheless, a triumphant, fulfilling experience.

'She's a girl!' I announced, incredulous, when James arrived. I had never imagined myself capable of producing a girl—a boy had been surprise enough. 'She weighs nine pounds.'

James picked her up. Her head was well-shaped, her skin soft as a flushed peach, no more flushed than if she had been running.

'We'll call her Ferelyth?' My question was politely affirmative rather than interrogatory. James went down to the Registrar's and had her called Janet. One look had shown him that she was not going to be a girl who would stand for singularity.

Hamish, not yet two, was brought to see her lying on my bed. Kneeling, steadying himself on his arms he kissed her carefully, tenderly. Not much later, during the War, there were times when he had to take care of her on his own.

When I got home and heard that Hitler had marched into Austria I broke the record of Strauss's "Morgen", sung by Elizabeth Schumann, over my knee, and buried Virginia Woolf in a tea-chest, for reading her was pure pleasure which I felt I should not allow myself in these terrible times.

I wrote the beginnings of a poem:

> With our firstborn
> Spain was invaded,
> On the day of our daughter's birth
> Austria was lost.

Michael Higgins, who had come in to give me a box of Black Magic chocolates, added:

> I fear to conceive again
> Lest Switzerland should fall.

It has its funny side; but gives the idea of what it was like to bear children then. I did not in fact "conceive again" till after the relief of Stalingrad in 1942, when for the first time there seemed to be a chance of beating the Nazis.

For the May Day procession in 1938 James built a platform on top of our van, and Hamish stood holding the rail dressed as a Republican soldier in a blue and scarlet sash and a forage cap, his small hand raised in the clenched-fist salute. Beside him swayed an equally diminutive girl dressed as the Spanish heroine, La Pasionaria. Our contingent moved off across Hammersmith Bridge at a snail's pace.

The Surrealists and the A.I.A. had put on a spectacular display: gigantic figures of Hitler, Mussolini and Franco weaved among the trades union banners and scarlet flags. There were tableaux mounted on vans; on one was a cage in which hung a skeleton, and a loudspeaker that played Spanish Republican records. A quartet of lifesize Chamberlains, Julian Trevelyan among them, wearing masks designed by F.E. MacWilliam, the sculptor, waved their rolled umbrellas, shouting 'Chamberlain must go!' and danced a minuet together when the procession halted.

But there was a note of defiance in our demonstration, in the slogans we shouted; an east wind blew ever more keenly as we wound our way to Hyde Park. The tide of the war was turning: the Republican forces were on the defensive on all fronts.

By the autumn of 1938 it was clear that the Spanish War was coming to an end. The Spanish War had been *our* war. The war to come we could have no decisive part in. We had seen what modern weaponry could do to civilians: now it was our turn to be the victims. There was still talk in Government circles, echoed among businessmen and filtered down to us through my father, of turning the war eastwards, of Germans being our natural allies. Since, in our philosophy, what was good for Russia was good for us, our continuing efforts were on her behalf also.

When the wind blew from the east on cool, grey summer days, a menacing gaseous smell bore down on us.

"For war is eating now. Waking, shaking off death," wrote Charles Madge. And William Empson: "It is the pain, it is the pain endures." And Stephen Spender's affirmation: "The palpable and obvious love of man for man". This was not too difficult for James, who loved almost everyone. But I didn't love many people. Marches, meetings, the Basque kids, cups of tea with the comrades—should I, if asked, have claimed a kind of comradely, communal love? No-one asked, least of all myself. No-one that I knew asked questions of themselves. Nor did we question each other.

"Save the Czechs!" James chalked on the pavement of Barnes, of Mortlake, of East Sheen. In East Sheen he was caught by the police. His look-out, an Elms brother made permanently punch-drunk in a boxing match, had failed to keep watch.

'These are tense, emotional times.' Thus the magistrate

commented, letting James off with a caution.

There was time to think, feeding Janet, sitting at the window looking out over the river at six o'clock on summer mornings. Here was peace, here was life continuing, in the rhythmic sucking at my breast, in the smell of milk and damp wool. Out there, across the water, wharves, cranes, barges caught the light as the sun shone up-river. I knew what was going to happen, how German planes following the river, as they had done in Spain, would darken our skies.

To mothers now, facing a different magnitude of horror so absolute as to be altogether different in scale, my fears cannot mean much. But remember that this was all we knew of annihilation.

So it was that at the time of the Munich crisis in September 1938, James took the van prospecting for a place to take us when war broke out. His War Office friend had promised to warn us when the outbreak of war was imminent.

The telephone rang: 'Go now.'

Within an hour or two Margaret Elms and Donald, Hamish and Janet and I drove out with James to a half-built housing estate in Metroland. The fortnight we spent there was as miserable as anything in the war to come. But routine life went on, the pram walks, the feeding times, "Children's Hour" on the wireless at tea-time, in a raw house with damp plaster walls, four hard chairs, beds and—a grim crematorium joke—a serving hatch.

During that time I ceased to care about saving the Czechs. My homesickness went back to my first separation from my mother at school. So when Chamberlain returned with the message, "Peace in our time", and we could go home, that was all I cared about, or Margaret either. We knew, of course, that there would not be peace; that this was only the beginning, and that war, when it came, would be the worse for us. But nothing interfered with our relief at seeing Barnes again, deceptively peaceful, unchanged. What was to have happened to Lotte? James and Frank Paterson, it was accepted, would have stayed to work, or to join the army, probably to die. But could we not have taken Lotte with us?

Now came the digging of trenches in the parks; and gas

masks were issued. The red and blue rubber of Hamish's obscene "Mickey Mouse" didn't fool him into trying it on. Janet was to be zipped into some all-enclosing coffin.

There was little time or inclination for meeting friends. But in the late autumn of 1938 we had dinner with Michael and Tanya Wickham in their Greenwich studio overlooking the river.

We ate seagulls' eggs and drank Chablis.

Tanya and I commiserated with each other: 'I'm getting so tired of banners in the hall,' I complained.

'Worse—pamphlets in the bed!'

There was, Michael remarked cautiously, a good deal in Marxist theory; it might not be entirely correct, he said, filling his pipe from a nineteenth-century Russian silver tobacco pouch. He went on to recall how Marx had predicted that the most highly industrialized countries would be the first to become socialist. Russia was not what Marx had predicted.

'But she soon will be,' I argued, thinking of the Five-Year Plan, the posters of youths and girls waving banners against a background of blast furnaces. Michael embarked on a brief critique of Russia's problems, agrarian, industrial, proletarian—not forgetting that she was surrounded by hostile powers who would never allow her to bring off what she had undertaken . . .

Having had enough of my limited grasp of political science, he went to the piano and played some Bach, not badly, I had to admit—for one was always half-hoping to catch Michael out. This reminded him of "Bach Goes to Town", a jazz version of a Bach fugue which he put on his gramophone with an enormous horn, the most perfect sound production then available. This beguiling, cheerful tune thereafter went with us everywhere.

In the spring of 1939 we drove down with Hamish to a derelict school near Petworth belonging to Ralph Parker. Here a number of his friends had been shut up for three days, eating, drinking and sleeping during the course of what had been, were still to be, the Rites of Spring. Until now the woods had been too damp and dripping for the rites to be celebrated more actively. But now they emerged, the Herberts, Jocelyn, her sister Chrystal, the Wickhams, the Higginses, Julian and Ursula and Janko Varda and a host of others, blinking in the forest twilight, huddling in their wraps. But now these coverings were cast aside, circles were formed, ritual dancing began, in the course of which Michael Higgins kissed me, a pleasing surprise. Then Julian, with a stag's antlers fixed to his head, galloped off among the silver birches, and the rest after him, like Comus' merry crew, knee-deep in soaking whortleberry bushes and dead bracken.

We went back to the van, James with Hamish on his shoulders, vaguely dispirited. It was too late, we felt, for the Rites of Spring.

(That must have been almost the last we saw of our Hammersmith friends before war started. But during the war the most surprising meeting occurred in the Red Lion Hotel, Truro. James, in the Intelligence Corps, walked into the bar to find Julian, a strange figure in battledress with his bunch of hair springing from under the side of his forage cap! No one could have been more unexpected, more joyously welcome. Julian, a camouflage officer, was there to lecture the troops on how to avoid detection from the air. He was very good at his job. 'You know when you are at a dance,' he would begin, 'and you're dancing with a gel wearing a black velvet frock?' (with a lascivious leer) 'And you put your hands on her bottom—down there, so . . . Your hand leaves a mark. That's what happens when you walk over wet grass—your tracks can be seen from the air.')

Towards the end of August I caught sight of an advertisement in the *New Statesman* for a furnished farmhouse, three guineas a week, near Hurstpierpoint in Sussex. Our lease of Riverview Gardens was coming to an end. We went and saw the place: the owners were returning to America. Without further thought we took Abbey Farm and prepared to move, storing our furniture.

XV
Abbey Farm

ABBEY FARM WAS built of flint, timbers and old brick, with a thatched roof that swept down at the back like a hooded cloak, protecting us from sou'westerlies. All round, beyond the low garden wall, were fields, and beyond them to the south rose up the Downs. Beyond the Downs lay the sea.

The rooms were long and low; upstairs the floors of wide polished planks sloped towards casement windows, and those windows, in that long, warm September, opened to the smell of lavender and late roses and a great bush of rosemary underneath our bedroom window. There were two crooked staircases, an attic, and at night the house smelled of apples.

These apples, when they ripened, were picked by Cherryman who not only did the garden and brought us in vegetables but worked in the house wearing a striped linen jacket. Cherryman was included in the rent. He did not care to be called "Mr" Cherryman.

After listening to Chamberlain's announcement at 11 a.m. on 3 September 1939: 'Consequently we are at war with Germany', I bicycled into Hurstpierpoint for blackout material, without enthusiasm, but with a sense that at last things were happening: for years we had been agitating for resistance against Hitler; now we had got what we wanted, albeit on poor terms. The sense of inevitability was not unlike pregnancy: nothing could stop it. The best one could do was to accept what was to come with active co-operation and as little fuss as possible. James had gone to London to join the army. He was posted to the Royal Fusiliers and came back in time for supper.

As to the flurry in the Communist Party, which changed overnight from supporting to opposing the war when the Russo-German pact was announced, James ignored it as did most of our C.P. friends. Our fruitless, crushing responsibility was over. We didn't need to write "Save the Czechs" on the pavement any more. The posters, the leaflets, the "literature" were gone, hastily crated with our furniture for storage. It was, though this I might not openly have admitted, a relief not to have to belong to the Communist Party any longer. Not because our political beliefs were altered: as Jessica Mitford has said, being in the Party changes your way of looking at things. But there was something unnatural about my friendships with the comrades, a political slant on all I felt and did, from which I felt released.

As to fear of the future, the fear of annihilation which I had felt a year ago, feeding Janet, watching the river, that was gone too. Abbey Farm was in a safe place, a reliance that must have been shared by the authorities since people were, for a time, evacuated to our area. Not that I was sanguine about the future. I had simply stopped being afraid of what might happen.

While writing this I remarked to James, 'I never thought we should win the war.' 'Didn't you?' he answered, 'I never thought we should lose.' This was news to both of us: at the time we never talked about it.

James came and went, tidying up his affairs at Morton Sundour. The war had come just in time to prevent his being sacked: he had stretched the paternalist benevolence of the directors to breaking point with his work for peace during office hours, designs for banners on the walls, his brazen use of the office number on his Arts Peace Campaign letter-paper. Now he could work out his time till he was called up.

I was made a billeting officer. In spite of the general air of camaraderie and patriotism, people of all classes were reluctant to have Jewish mothers and babies. We took the Bronsteins in at Abbey Farm. There seemed to be a lot of Bronsteins, who came from the East End of London. Mrs Bronstein and her under-fives were soon joined by more of her family. She was dark with gold earrings like a gypsy and hardly spoke English. Her husband did the talking. There was room for us all at Abbey Farm, and though the large kitchen which they took over was dark, they seemed content and self-sufficient; before long, they had become part of the place. There was no electricity; they cooked on the coal range, from which floated forth interesting foreign odours of sesame seeds and sunflower oil and unidentified ingredients. We managed on Calor gas in the scullery.

Increasingly I became numbed towards the outside world, living enclosed within the walls, in the garden where the babies played, slept and ate, growing browner with every cloudless day. These two, in their tenderness, their vulnerability, their beauty, drew out of me feelings I did not know I possessed, with a commitment that I could not be sure of sustaining.

I had never lived in the country before except for visits to Windrush. Living where we did, during the richest and most beguiling of all seasons, in summer weather which seemed unending, we moved, drunk as bees, through light, leaves and shadows, under fruit trees, among purple autumn flowers, lavender, Michaelmas daisies that harboured Red Admiral butterflies, scarlet and yellow dahlias, white, frail-stalked Japanese anemones like small moons. We walked about the meadows where cows stood knee-deep in rich pasture; we watched the corn being cut, followed the laden floats to great barns where evening light shafted through golden dust into the dark interior.

Towards evening when the children were in bed I walked away through water meadows, up chalk paths and along the crest of the Downs to Clayton Mill, running barefoot over cropped grass, free as I had not been since the children's birth.

When James was there, at week-ends, we went further afield. With Hamish and Janet tied into little seats we bicycled about the countryside.

As September deepened into autumn every night and day brought change. The harvest moon, rising, flooded the stubble fields with yellow then white light. In the mornings from our bedroom window we saw the backs of cows like hippopotami, their stumpy legs hidden in mist. Every day was new, seen as though for the first time. We picked mushrooms for breakfast, came in dew-drenched. Spiders' webs held droplets, eye-dazzling as the sun grew stronger. October brought the glory of turning leaves. During the day bonfires burned; night sharpened in our nostrils.

Halfway through October, James was called up and went away for training.

Still nothing was quite real, that is, all reality was contained in Abbey Farm, stretched no further than I could walk on the Downs. Though I made plans, they were not felt as events which were going to happen.

We could not stay on at Abbey Farm. There was talk of the South Downs being "our first line of defence". The evacuees were moved. And with James's money as a private soldier we should have to move anyway. I arranged to go to a house in Oxfordshire where the teacher who had run Hamish's nursery school was taking some of her pupils whose mothers had chosen to do "war work", learning to drive ambulances and working in ministries. There were to be eight or ten children, none older than four, mostly three, and one of two. I, without qualifications, was to be cook-housekeeper. The decision made, I gave it no further thought until such time as James could come back and take us there.

Summer weather, long-drawn-out, gave way unwillingly to the end of autumn. Leaves swirled about our heads, Hamish ran about catching at them as cats spring at low-flying birds. Cherryman, who trimmed and filled the lamps, now lit them and carried them through the rooms before he left to go home to his family. I ate my supper on my knee listening to the radio; finished my story, *Pension Bellevue*, later published in John Lehmann's *New Writing*, and began another also published by John Lehmann. I loved the nights, the silence, owls calling in the misty woods, stars clear above the mist. And always the long protective shoulder of the Downs, dark and then paling, glowing with light as the moon rose. Now it was the hunter's moon riding high, cold, clear, bringing a touch of frost.

One day James came home, walking across the fields from the station. I'm not one to cry "properly", though my eyes too readily fill with tears for romantic or sentimental reasons. But when he came close I burst into tears. For the first time he was wearing battledress and a forage cap. It was the shock of seeing him, I said, feeling the tickly, hairy cloth, the high collar up to his chin. He had two days' leave. He had come to help me pack up and drive us to Kidlington.

And now, for the first time, it came home to me that we were really going to be on our own, the children and I.

That night I thought of the early days of our marriage.

'When we left London,' I said, 'I thought things would be the same.' I meant, and James knew this, the same as they had been in Little Sussex Place.

We clung to each other. 'How could they be the same,' he said, 'how can things ever be the same again?'

Coda

I HAD INTENDED to end my memories at the beginning of World War II because, as a friend said, 'It was a watershed for us all.' But one or two people who have read it said they were left asking: 'What happened next?' My publisher, too, found the ending abrupt and suggested using a musical term, a coda.

Writing about us both has been, in some sort, like writing about the grandchildren, since our eldest is now older than we were when we married. I should like to have told those two, lying in their farmhouse room smelling of apples and rosemary, how, as James probably sensed, nothing is ever the same again, and how unadventurous, how stagnant life would be if it were. Life for us has been one surprise after another—some that might have been foreseen and prevented! We have gone on for the most part as we began, not learning much from experience, breasting each wave as it came, diving through or engulfed, tumbled over with stones and currents, surfacing, "being lived our life".

Recently, the children gave us a party to celebrate our joint seventieth birthday. Looking down Hamish's long dinner table, nothing surprises me more than our possessing nine grandchildren! Where now is Peter Pan? Whither is fled the little orphan girl?

James, yes: sitting at the far end, he is a natural grandfather. Well, I am a grandmother. Grandparenthood is a source of love and pride unalloyed by guilt.

There they are, all ages, with their parents—and they are, believe me, quite exceptionally beautiful, handsome, talented, not one dullard in the lot—there they are among the roses and the candles, flushed and shining, fair heads laid against the dark. There too are my sister Ferelyth, Bill and their brood; and old friends, the Usbornes, the Wickhams, the Trevelyans and many who came later than the close of my story in 1939. Leaning back, I think: we have survived, most of us have survived through five decades at once the most hopeful and promising, and the most terrible in the history of mankind. Promising because we have within our grasp the knowledge, the power to end much misery, poverty, disease, perhaps war itself, and to bring about the socialist society which James and I naïvely, but not wrongly, believed to be possible and necessary. Terrible because we have misused our knowledge; we have learnt nothing about ourselves or how to live together. Envy and greed we may recognize, though projected on to our enemies. But of what might yet save us, what Cecil Day Lewis wrote of as "the disinterested movements of moral fervour and intellectual curiosity, the spontaneous springings of Mercy, Pity, Peace and Love"—of these, of their source, we understand almost nothing. We hold in our hands like toys the instruments of our destruction. W. H. Auden's words, "we must love one another or die", now have a literal, an apocalyptic truth.

In 1945 two French girls who had grown up working in the Resistance Movement were sent to stay with us. Of the Liberation they said: 'We were students, we walked through the streets singing.'

'What did you sing?'

'*Nous chantions le lendemain.*'

Lord, let our children go on singing, I pray.

The speeches are done, the crumbs cleared, the company push back their chairs, change places. Rab, the youngest, has fallen asleep with his head on his father's knee.

'What happened next?' asked Lucy, one of our grandchildren, speaking as I thought about her grandfather. 'What happened after the war?'

'More or less as you heard,' I replied. For as one speaker had said, James returned to publishing and, for all the ups and downs and reverses, has spent almost all his working life doing what he loves best—publishing books. 'That and sailing,' I said.

'No—I mean you—what happened to you after the war?'

I had been reminiscing with Dick Usborne and others about the war years.

'During the war years you had your first two stories published,' said Lucy, 'and the children got whooping cough, the Germans were going to be dropped on Inkpen Beacon only they never came, a flaming Heinkel flew over the house and you put the children under their beds, the Travelling Theatre came to Newbury and you went about with them acting plays in Corn Exchanges and army camps, your first novel was published, Robert was born—it wasn't half a bad war one way and another, not half a bad war! But what happened next?'

'That's difficult,' I said, 'for a long time it was difficult. I don't want to talk about it.'

Lucy laid her cheek against mine, said no more and went away.

What happened was that, on VE Day, I collapsed into a complete breakdown. Edith took Robert and cared for him—the other two were at school—till James was allowed home on compassionate leave.

It has always puzzled me how people can write—and interestingly too—about their own madness. Mine was a monotonous treadmill, an unending torment of fear. Worst of all, I could not write. But throughout I continued to mind, with a vestige of sanity loved, minded about the children; and holding fast to this thread of common sense I was helped to find a psychoanalyst who, after years of patient, skilled work, restored me to a life that is the more precious for being still precarious, felt to be undeserved, sometimes difficult to believe in. After a while I began to write again, first criticism and reviewing, then children's stories, though not as I had once hoped. During those years I could be at home with the children rather than away in an institution; and was able to help James, whose loving tolerance during this time was unfailing, with his own publishing firm.

But that is all long past.

Sitting on at the table, I thought that this, our celebration, was as good, as true and as loving and blessed a time as ever I remember, netting up our years together, the fulfilment, the contentment we have come to.

The candles are out, our guests departed, the children gathered for a last goodbye.

'Come,' says James.

We put on our coats and together come home.

INDEX